It's Not That Simple

Euthanasia and Assisted Suicide Today

First published in 2015 by
The deVeber Institute for Bioethics and Social Research
15 Oakdale Road, Suite 215
Toronto M3N 1W7
Ontario, Canada

Reprinted in 2015.

www.deveber.org   Email: bioethics@deveber.org   Phone: 416-256-0555

Library and Archives Canada Cataloguing in Publication

Echlin, Jean, author
        It's not that simple: euthanasia and assisted suicide
        today / Jean Echlin, Ian Gentles.

ISBN 978-0-920453-37-7 (paperback)

1. Euthanasia. 2. Assisted suicide. Gentles, Ian, author
II. deVeber Institute for Bioethics and Social Research, issuing
body III. Title. IV. Title: It's Not That Simple.

R726.I87 2015   179.7   C2015-906767-7

Printed in Canada

It's Not That Sim

Euthanasia and
Assisted Suicide To

Jean Echlin
Ian Gentles

With the assistance of Adam Giancola, Ju
Christina Holmquist, Conor Sweel
and Lisa Hamilton.

The deVeber Institute for Bioe
and Social Research
2015

It's Not That Simple:

Euthanasia and Assisted Suicide Today

Table of Contents

Preface and Acknowledgements — i

Chapter 1: **Introduction** — 1

Chapter 2: **The Supreme Court Decision on Assisted Suicide** — 9
With assistance from Adam Giancola

Chapter 3: **The State of the Law throughout the World** — 39
With assistance from Julia Giancola

Chapter 4: **The Experience of Jurisdictions which have Legalized Assisted Suicide or Euthanasia** — 63
With assistance from Christina Holmquist

Chapter 5: **Why Patients Request Euthanasia and Assisted Suicide** — 99
With assistance from Conor Sweetman

Chapter 6: **Quality of Life with Palliative Care Not Euthanasia** — 113
With assistance from Lisa Hamilton

Conclusion — 153

References — 161

Glossary — 181

Index — 189

Preface and Acknowledgements

It's Not That Simple comes at a critical moment in Canada's history. The longstanding ban on assisted suicide has been lifted and our government now confronts the challenge of framing a law that respects the ruling of the Supreme Court on 6th February 2015, at the same time that it furnishes maximum protection for vulnerable people, and upholds the freedom of religion and conscience of not only individual doctors and nurses, but also of hospitals and palliative care institutions, whose principles do not permit them to participate in "assisted dying", or any other form of euthanasia. Shortly after the Supreme Court announced its ruling in the Carter case the deVeber Institute decided to publish a book analyzing the implications of this ruling. Our book outlines the legal ramifications of the epochal decision of the Supreme Court, as well as the effects it will have on the Canadian healthcare system. We conclude our analysis with a consideration of the positive alternatives to assisted suicide – skilled, compassionate palliative care, including adequate pain management. There is no reason why any citizen approaching the end of life should be denied such care. It has been demonstrated again and again that those who are given proper palliative care rarely request assisted suicide.

It's Not That Simple could not have been finished without the help of many people. Our summer student interns, Adam Giancola, Christina Holmquist, Julia Giancola, Conor Sweetman, Lisa Hamilton, and

Martha McNeely, carried out an immense amount of research, writing, checking of references and other essential tasks.

Our special thanks go to Professors Keith Cassidy and Elizabeth Ring Cassidy for hosting a weekend symposium to develop the book in July 2015 at their Academy in Barry's Bay. The speakers and participants at the symposium provided much valuable information and many insights that were of tremendous help to the authors.

We are immensely grateful to Professor Margaret Somerville of McGill University's faculties of Law and Medicine, Deborah Zeni, MD, Paul Zeni, MD, Will Johnston, MD, Paul Ranalli, MD, and Alex Schadenberg who read the manuscript and helped us correct errors. Hugh Scher clarified several legal issues for us. Paul Broughton and Aimée Rochard provided invaluable publication and editorial support, and Bjoern Arthurs designed the cover.

We are profoundly grateful to the Edward Jackman Foundation, as well as many individual donors, whose generosity made the book possible. Special thanks also go to Martha Crean and Lorraine McCallum who have worked tirelessly to perfect the book. Kathy Matusiak supplied indispensable administrative assistance, and oversaw the preparation of the book from beginning to end. Finally, we gratefully acknowledge the commitment and labour of our Board of Directors, Advisors, Associates, and supporters for all their help and encouragement along the way.

Chapter 1

Introduction

On a balmy Friday evening in the early summer of 2015 the Institute of Medical Science at the University of Toronto held what it called "A Thought-Provoking Conversation on the Future of Physician-Assisted Suicide". Four experts representing different shades on the spectrum of opinion debated one another and answered questions. The audience comprised 200 or more medical professionals, medical students and members of the general public. At the beginning of the evening they were polled on the question, "Do you think Canada is ready for physician-assisted suicide?" Their response was Yes by a margin of 51 to 49 per cent. Two hours later, having heard all sides of the question, and reflected on reports about the distress of many medical professionals over the prospect of having to administer lethal pills and injections, and about how many elderly patients were anxiously asking their doctors what the recent legalization of assisted suicide would mean for them, a significant proportion of the audience changed their mind. Having thought seriously about the ramifications of the Supreme Court ruling, only 28 per cent were still convinced that Canada was ready for physician-assisted suicide; 72 per cent thought it was not.[1]

---

1   "Beyond the Debate: A Thought-Provoking Conversation on the Future of Physician-Assisted Suicide", Institute of Medical Science. Isabel Bader Theatre, University of Toronto. June 19, 2015.

Why public opinion is unreliable

This shift of opinion over the course of one evening on the part of a large group of well-informed and highly-qualified people, illustrates why public opinion polls --which consistently show massive support for the legalization of physician-assisted suicide -- are not necessarily the best guide in the formulation of public policy. Still less ought the shifting sands of public opinion to have influenced the Supreme Court of Canada in deciding on the constitutionality of physician-assisted suicide. Yet the Court implicitly admitted that public opinion had been a significant factor in its decision.[2]

The many consequences of the Supreme Court ruling

There will be many ramifications to the elimination of the Criminal Code prohibitions against assisted suicide. Among them will be the legacy of sorrow and distress that will be left to the families and loved ones of those who opt to have themselves killed. Those close to them will be haunted by the question of what they might have done to steer their loved one away from suicide. Many doctors and nurses who have dedicated their lives to healing bodies and minds, and preserving lives, will also suffer great mental anguish when they are called upon now to destroy life.

The healing vocation of medical professionals will be corrupted by the practice of assisted suicide.

---

2   *Carter v Canada*, 2015 SCC 15, [2015] 1 SCR 331. See paragraph 28, which refers to "changes in the social and factual landscape over the past 20 years".

Equally, many sick, frail, vulnerable, disabled and elderly people, will find their lives at risk as never before. Those who doubt this prediction should consider the evidence we advance in Chapter Four of the extent to which this has already happened in the Netherlands and Belgium. Close family members and those with power of attorney will also face unprecedented temptations. The need to save on expensive medical bills, or the desire to hasten the arrival of a long-awaited inheritance will pose great temptations once physician-assisted suicide becomes an easy option. A physician specializing in geriatric care recently said to one of the authors, "I run into this all the time. The relatives of elderly patients often ask me, "'Doctor, *can't you do something…*'[to hasten the patient's death]?"

The Expert Panel to recommend legislation on assisted suicide

In July of this year the Federal Government announced the appointment of a three-member expert panel to make recommendations for dealing with the Supreme Court's lifting of the prohibition against assisted suicide and euthanasia chaired by Dr Harvey Max Chochinov, who holds a Canada Research Chair in palliative care at the University of Manitoba. He has pioneered "dignity-preserving care" – ways of making palliative care patients feel valued. Committee member Dr, Catherine Frazee, former Chief Human Rights Commissioner of Ontario and an expert in disability studies, has said that state-sanctioned assisted death raises questions of how far personal freedoms should extend.

> At the heart of this debate, we must choose between competing visions of our social fabric. Shall we uncritically submit to the voracious demands of individual liberty no matter what the social cost? Or shall we agree that there are limits to individual freedom, limits that serve us all when we are vulnerable and in decline? [3]

The awareness of these two members of the expert panel of the great perils of unrestricted legalization of physician-assisted suicide gives grounds for hope that the law, when it is eventually adopted, will feature stringent safeguards against abuse. On the other hand, as we demonstrate in this book, all the safeguards in the world are not proof against abuse, and will not necessarily protect significant numbers of people from being euthanized without their knowledge or consent. The third member of the panel is Benoit Pelletier, an expert in constitutional law at the University of Ottawa.

The religious and conscience rights of doctors, nurses and healthcare institutions

Another question raised by the Supreme Court's ruling is the rights of medical professionals who have religious or conscientious objections to euthanasia and assisted suicide. Will they be entitled not only to abstain from these procedures, but also to decline to refer patients for them? Within the medical profession there has been strong pressure to force physicians with religious or conscientious objections to refer patients

---

3   Quoted by Sharon Kirkey, "Panel to review assisted dying". *National Post*, July 18, 2015, p. A1.

who request assisted suicide to others willing to provide the service. The argument is that if the service is legal then all physicians, whatever their religious or ethical position, have a duty to make that service available to patients who want it. This argument demonstrates, on the part of those who make it, what amounts to willful obliviousness to religious freedom, freedom of conscience and freedom of professional judgment. Consider the following analogy. What if female genital mutilation were a legal medical service, as it still is in some countries today? Would it show respect for a physician with religious, medical or ethical objections to the practice to obligate him or her to refer patients for that service, just because it was legal?

Perhaps helpfully, the Canadian Medical Association, at its annual convention in August 2015 found that the greatest support among attendees was for the option that limited a physician's duty to providing "complete information on all options and [to] advise on how to access a separate central information, counselling, and referral service".[4] Any move to force doctors to refer for assisted suicide or euthanasia would undoubtedly be appealed to the Supreme Court on the ground that it violated article 2 a) of the Canadian Charter of Rights and Freedoms which guarantees freedom of conscience and religion.[5]

Almost overlooked in the debate over freedom of conscience and religion is the freedom of institutions

---

4   25 Aug. 2015. For this information we thank Sharon Koke, who was in attendance at the CMA Convention on that day.
5   Constitution Act, 1982. Part I, Canadian Charter of Rights and Freedoms. http://laws-lois.justice.gc.ca/eng/const/page-15.html

such as Catholic hospitals to follow their founding principles and refrain from destroying innocent human life. This freedom has been recognized when it comes to abortion. But the government of the Province of Quebec shows no such sensitivity in its Bill 52, now An Act Respecting End-of-life Care, due to come into force on 15 December 2015. [6] It assumes that "medically assisted dying" is part of the "continuum of healthcare". While doctors with religious or conscience objections to assisted suicide will not be compelled to participate in "assisted dying", they will be expected to refer their patients to physicians willing to offer the service. Similarly, while palliative-care hospices will not be required to offer "medically assisted dying", other institutions such as hospitals, will be expected to carry out state policy. This policy, if enforced, could result in the shutting down of Catholic hospitals.[7]

The Quebec government has already demonstrated that it will not wait for the recommendations of the Federal Government's Expert Panel. At the beginning of September it announced that Quebec doctors will shortly be given standardized kits with which to end the lives of patients seeking euthanasia.[8] This "service" will be available to anyone judged to be in "constant and unbearable physical or psychological pain."

---

6   *An Act Respecting End-of-Life Care*, RSQ c S-32.0001, s 1; http://www.assnat.qc.ca/en/travaux-parlementaires/projets-loi/projet-loi-52-40-1.html

7   *An Act Respecting End-of-Life Care*, Chap III.9.

8 | Sharon Kirkey, "Quebec MDs to get euthanasia packages", *National Post*, Sept. 1, 2015, p. A1.

The perils for vulnerable people: lessons from Belgium and the Netherlands

The Quebec law is modelled on legislation already in place in Belgium. It shows little interest in the perils that legislation poses to vulnerable people. It demonstrates indifference to the virtual abandonment of palliative care that has been documented in the Netherlands. That country now has a total of only 70 palliative-care beds, in contrast to the many thousands of such beds in Britain, which has not legalized euthanasia. [9] Nor have the Quebec policy makers evidently taken any account of Theo Boer, who was involved in developing and implementing the Dutch legislation legalizing euthanasia. He warns, "we were wrong, terribly wrong", and urges other countries not to make the same mistake.[10] Nor apparently have they read the testimony of Lord McColl, of the British House of Lords Select Committee on Euthanasia. After returning from a fact-finding mission to the Netherlands he stated, "Our visit convinced me that euthanasia is impossible to police and will be abused."[11]

The purpose of our book is to show that there is substance to these warnings, and that our policy makers will ignore them at their peril. But our book

---

9   H. Matthews. Better Palliative Care Could Cut Euthanasia. BMJ 12 Dec.1998; 317 (1773), p. 1613. Britain (the U.K.) has approximately four times the population of the Netherlands.

10   Quoted by Steve Doughty. "Don't Make Our Mistake: As Assisted Suicide Goes to Lords, Dutch Watchdog Who Once Backed Euthanasia Warns UK of 'Slippery Slope' to Mass Deaths. Daily Mail; July 9, 2014.

11   Quoted in Matthews. Better Palliative Care Could Cut Euthanasia, p. 1613.

has an additional, equally important purpose. We also intend to show that if there is good palliative care, and compassionate attention to human pain in all its dimensions, the demand for assisted suicide will be greatly reduced.[12]

---

12   See for example, C. Marijke et al. Requests for euthanasia and physician assisted suicide and the availability and application of palliative options. Palliative and Supportive Care 2006; 4:399-406; Marit Karlsson et al. Suffering and euthanasia: a qualitative study of dying cancer patients' perspectives. Support Care Cancer 2012; 20: 1065-71.

Chapter 2 *

The Supreme Court Decision on Assisted Suicide

Introduction

On 6 February 2015 the Supreme Court of Canada unleashed a constitutional hurricane.[1] Defying the clearly-expressed will of Parliament, sidestepping its previous decision of only 22 years ago, and flying in the face of many recommendations from advisory bodies, including those of the medical profession, the Court nullified the longstanding prohibition on assisted suicide. It justified overriding the Criminal Code of Canada by reference to recent shifts in public opinion and conflicting evidence from the social sciences. The Court also declared that the autonomy of the individual was a paramount constitutional principle, trumping considerations of the public safety.

In the wake of the pronouncement by the Supreme Court this chapter addresses the issues that the federal government will be obliged to consider when it drafts new legislation on medical aid in dying, meaning physician-assisted suicide. We begin by outlining the judicial history preceding the Supreme Court's decision of 6 February 2015. Then we discuss the recommendations of various expert bodies that have studied euthanasia and physician-assisted suicide. Next

---

* *Chapter 2 written with the assistance of Adam Giancola.*
1   *Carter v Canada*, 2015 SCC 15, [2015] 1 SCR 331[*Carter*].

we analyze the implications of Quebec's Bill 52 legalizing physician-assisted suicide or "assisted dying" in that province. Subsequently we discuss how completely the Supreme Court has disregarded the repeatedly expressed will of Parliament. After this we discuss the "test" laid down by the Supreme Court in its ruling and the possible areas of ambiguity that lie within this "test." Further, we consider some of the questions left unanswered by the Supreme Court, and their implications. Finally, we discuss some of the protections that may or may not be available to patients when making end-of-life decisions under an assisted suicide regime. We conclude with a broader analysis of the dangers of imprudent legislation, and its possible consequences.

The Sue Rodriguez case of 1993

It is worth recalling that in 1993 the Court had made it clear in *Rodriguez v British Columbia*[2] that "the societal concern with preserving life and protecting the vulnerable renders a blanket prohibition preferable to a law which might not adequately prevent abuse."[3] Sue Rodriguez was suffering from ALS or Lou Gehrig's Disease. Despite her plea for assistance to end her own life, the Court decided that the social good was of higher importance than relieving the suffering of one individual. In the words of the longstanding legal dictum, "hard cases make bad law."

Four years later in *R v Latimer*[4] the Court again upheld the Criminal Code provisions against euthanasia

---

2   [1993] 3 SCR 519 [*Rodriguez*].

3   *Rodriguez, see* note 2, p. 605.

4   [1997] 1 SCR 217.

and assisted suicide. Robert Latimer, a Manitoba farmer, had taken it into his own hands to euthanize his twelve-year-old daughter by gassing her to death in the cab of his truck. Why did he do this? Because, in his judgement, her various physical disabilities rendered her life not worth living. The court upheld his conviction for second-degree murder, pointing out that he had no moral or legal right to pass judgment on the worth of another person's life.

The Special Senate Committee on euthanasia and assisted suicide

In the aftermath of the Court's decision in *Rodriguez*, a Special Senate Committee on Euthanasia and Assisted Suicide was struck to consider the issue of end-of-life care. Its report, *Of Life and Death,* recommended that "no amendments be made to the offence of counselling suicide under subsection 241(a) of the Criminal Code" and that "subsection 241(b) of the Code also remain intact."[5] The majority also recommended that all forms of euthanasia (voluntary, involuntary, and non-voluntary) remain offences under the Criminal Code.[6] Five years later a Senate subcommittee was asked to study the fate of the recommendations set out in *Of Life and Death.* In June 2000, the subcommittee published *Quality End-of-life Care: The Right of Every Canadian.* This Report warned that "the principles, expertise, and medical infrastructure required for the care of people facing death were evolving far too slowly."[7]

---

5   The Special Senate Committee on Euthanasia and Assisted Suicide, *Of Life and Death - Final Report* (June 1995); http://www.parl.gc.ca/Content/SEN/Committee/351/euth/rep/lad-tc-e.htm

6   Special Senate Committee, *Of Life and Death.*

7   Senate of Canada, *Quality End-of-Life Care: The Right of Every Canadian,* Report of the Subcommittee to Update *Of Life and Death* (June 2000), p. 3.

The Collège des médecins du Québec

In 2009, the Collège des médecins du Québec published a discussion paper entitled *Physicians, Appropriate Care and the Debate on Euthanasia.* The Collège argued that "[a] new sensitivity is clearly perceivable within the population and the medical profession, advocating that we stop denying the existence of these difficult situations and that we openly discuss the various options facing us."[8] The Collège further suggested that this "new sensitivity" was not inconsistent with the spirit of the Code of Ethics of Quebec Physicians. Section 58 of that Code stipulates that "[a] physician must, when the death of a patient appears to him to be inevitable, act so that the death occurs with dignity. He must also ensure that the patient obtains appropriate support and relief."[9] The Collège found that appropriate end-of-life care "must be proportioned, personalized and appropriate and not just technically feasible."[10] Within its definition of appropriate end-of-life care, the Collège declared that "the question of euthanasia must be integrated as a part of appropriate end-of-life care as soon as possible."[11]

---

8   Collège des médecins du Québec, *Physicians, Appropriate Care and the Debate on Euthanasia – A Reflection* (October 2009), p. 2 [*Collège des médecins*]; http://www.cmq.org/en/Medias/Profil/Commun/ Nouvelles/2009/~/media/208E2B537FB144FAAE33DEB458D3AA90. ashx?91027

9   *Code of Ethics of Quebec Physicians*, c M-9, r 17, s 58; http:// www2.publicationsduquebec.gouv.qc.ca/dynamicSearch/telecharge. php?type=3&file=/M_9/M9R17_A.HTM

10   Collège des médecins, *see* note 8, p. 4.

11   Collège des médecins, *see* note 8, p. 7.

The Canadian Medical Association's opposition to euthanasia

This opening the door to euthanasia was in stark contrast to the policy of the Canadian Medical Association, which at its annual meetings, had continued to affirm that no physician should participate in euthanasia or assisted suicide.[12] Under intense pressure the CMA modified its policy at its June 2014 meeting. Recognizing "the prerogative of society to decide whether the laws dealing with euthanasia and assisted death should be changed", it nevertheless upheld the right of all physicians to refuse to participate in these procedures. It went on to advocate that "efforts to broaden the availability of palliative care in Canada should be intensified." It also expressed serious concern that "the interests of those at risk of attempting suicide for other reasons must be safeguarded. Suicide-prevention programs should be maintained and strengthened where necessary." It added the cogent observation that attempted suicide "is often the result of temporary depression or unhappiness. *Society rightly supports efforts to prevent suicide, and physicians are expected to provide life-support measures to people who have attempted suicide*"[13] [Emphasis added]. This can hardly be characterized as a ringing endorsement of the legalization of euthanasia and assisted suicide.

---

12   Martha Butler, Marlisa Tiedemann, Julia Nicol, Dominique Valiquet, *Euthanasia and Assisted Suicide in Canada*. Library of Parliament Research Publications, Background Paper No.2010-68-E. February 2013; http://www.parl.gc.ca/Content/LOP/ResearchPublications/2010-68-e.htm#a11

13   Canadian Medical Association, *Euthanasia and Assisted Death (Update 2014)*, p. 3. http://www.cma.ca/Assets/assets-library/document/en/advocacy/EOL/CMA_Policy_Euthanasia_Assisted%20Death_PD15-02-e.pdf

The report of the Select Committee on Dying with Dignity to the Quebec Legislature

Choosing to follow a radically different route, in 2009 the Quebec Legislature appointed the Select Committee on Dying with Dignity, and assigned it the task of hearing submissions from across the province and making new recommendations for end-of-life care. After hearing over 250 submissions -- the majority opposed to euthanasia and assisted suicide -- the committee published its report in March 2012. It pushed for reforms in palliative care, palliative sedation, advance medical directives, end-of-life care, and medical aid in dying.[14] It further urged the enactment of legislation that would give persons the ability to obtain "medical aid in dying" [assisted suicide] when the following criteria were met:

1. The person is a Québec resident according to the Health Insurance Act;

2. The person is an adult able to consent to treatment under the law;

3. The person himself requests medical aid in dying after making a free and informed decision;

4. The person is suffering from a serious, incurable disease;

---

14 **Martha Butler, Marlisa Tiedemann, Julia Nicol, Dominique Valiquet,** *Euthanasia and Assisted Suicide in Canada.* Library of Parliament Research Publications, Background Paper ± N°.2010-68-E. February 2013; http://www.parl.gc.ca/Content/LOP/ResearchPublications/2010-68-e.htm#a11

5. The person is in an advanced state of weakening capacities, with no chance of improvement;
6. The person has constant and unbearable physical or psychological suffering that cannot be eased under conditions he deems tolerable.[15]

The Royal Society of Canada's recommendations

Prior to the publication of this report, the Royal Society of Canada had also contributed recommendations for end-of-life care in a report entitled *End-of-Life Decision Making*. Released in November 2011, this report sketched a new landscape for end-of-life care in Canada. Besides advocating the continued improvement of palliative care services, the report called for "a permissive yet carefully regulated and monitored system" to allow for physician-assisted dying.[16] In its final recommendations the report urged amendment of the criminal law to permit assisted suicide and euthanasia as end-of-life options for Canadians. Unlike Québec's Select Committee on Dying with Dignity, however, this report did not provide explicit wording for a Criminal Code amendment. Nonetheless, the Royal Society recognized that the federal government was in the best position to legislate on assisted suicide and euthanasia in order to ensure uniform practice across the country.[17]

---

15   National Assembly, *Select Committee: Dying With Dignity Report* (March 2012), p. 80; http://www.dyingwithdignity.ca/database/files/library/Quebec_death_with_dignity_report.pdf

16   Udo Schuklenk et al., *End-of-Life Decision Making*, The Royal Society of Canada (November 2011), p. 9; http://rsc-src.ca/sites/default/files/pdf/RSCEndofLifeReport2011_EN_Formatted_FINAL.pdf

17   Schuklenk, *End-of-Life Decision Making*, p. 96.

In response to the recommendations of the Select Committee on Dying with Dignity and the Royal Society of Canada, the Quebec government appointed an expert panel to determine how to implement those recommendations.[18] In January 2013 the panel released its final report, advocating that assisted suicide be made part of the "continuum of care" offered by the medical profession. Rather than waiting for the Federal Parliament to alter the Criminal Code, the report took the view that assisted suicide "could fall into provincial jurisdiction over health care delivery."[19]

Quebec's Bill 52 legalizes assisted suicide

In line with this view, on June 5th 2014 the Quebec government passed Bill 52, *An Act Respecting End-of-Life Care*. The bill incorporates verbatim in its first paragraph the language of the government's expert panel report:

> The Act establishes the rights of such patients as well as the organization of and a framework for end-of-life care so that everyone may have access, throughout the *continuum of care*, to

---

18   Jean-Pierre Ménard et al., *Mettre en œuvre les recommandations de la Commission spéciale de l'Assemblée nationale sur la question de mourir dans la dignité: Rapport du Comité de juristes experts* (January 2013); http://www.dyingwithdignity.ca/database/files/library/rapport_comite_juristes_experts.pdf; **Martha Butler, Marlisa Tiedemann, Julia Nicol, Dominique Valiquet,** *Euthanasia and Assisted Suicide in Canada*. Library of Parliament Research Publications, Background Paper N°.2010-68-E. February 2013; http://www.parl.gc.ca/Content/LOP/ResearchPublications/2010-68-e.htm#a11

19   **Martha Butler, Marlisa Tiedemann, Julia Nicol, Dominique Valiquet,** *Euthanasia and Assisted Suicide in Canada*. Library of Parliament Research Publications, Background Paper‡ N°.2010-68-E. February 2013; http://www.parl.gc.ca/Content/LOP/ResearchPublications/2010-68-e.htm#a11

quality care that is appropriate to their needs, including prevention and relief of suffering [Emphasis added].[20]

The Act authorizes a patient to obtain medical aid in dying if he or she satisfies the following criteria:

> (1) is an insured person within the meaning of the Health Insurance Act (chapter A-29);
>
> (2) is of full age and capable of giving consent to care;
>
> (3) is at the end of life;
>
> (4) suffers from a serious and incurable illness;
>
> (5) is in an advanced state of irreversible decline in capability; and
>
> (6) experiences constant and unbearable physical or psychological suffering which cannot be relieved in a manner the patient deems tolerable.[21]

For these people Quebec's Act legalizes both physician-assisted suicide and euthanasia – lethal injections and "terminal palliative sedation". Confusingly, "palliative sedation" currently means maximal sedation to control symptoms without intending to kill the patient. Quebec's Act changes this. By adding the word "terminal" the Act makes is clear that in future the purpose of this type of sedation will be to kill the patient.

---

20   *An Act Respecting End-of-Life Care*, RSQ c S-32.0001, s 1 [*Act*]; http://www.assnat.qc.ca/en/travaux-parlementaires/projets-loi/projet-loi-52-40-1.html
21   *Act, see* note 20, s 26.

Particularly worthy of note is that both Quebec's Act and the test laid out in the Supreme Court's decision in *Carter* define the suffering of the patient subjectively, such that the individual patient's tolerance for suffering determines their eligibility for medical assistance in dying. This language may prove to broaden unduly the circumstances that fall within the scope of the legislation.

While Quebec's Law only precedes the Supreme Court's decision in *Carter* by a few months, it may point to the way in which that decision is implemented at the federal level. One example has to do with the actual practice of assisted suicide, and the discretion that is left in the hands of the medical profession for end-of-life decision-making. In April 2015 the National Post reported a study showing mass confusion among Quebec doctors about what practices are permissible under the province's new legislation.[22] Going much farther than merely overriding the Criminal Code provisions against assisted suicide, Quebec's legislation assumes that assisted suicide is an integral component of healthcare. In the words of the Act, medical aid in dying is part of the "continuum of care,"[23] rather than an exceptional remedy. It remains to be seen whether the federal government will indeed adopt the same approach when it drafts national legislation.

---

22   Sharon Kirkey, "Confusion over euthanasia: third of doctors wrongly believe it's family's call, Quebec poll finds" *National Post* (April 2015); http://news.nationalpost.com/news/canada/confusion-over-euthanasia-third-of-doctors-wrongly-believe-its-familys-call-quebec-poll-finds

23   *Act, see* note 20, s 1.

Limited conscience rights for individuals but none for institutions that object to the Quebec law

The Quebec law calls for "end-of-life" care to be provided to every person who qualifies for it. This includes both palliative care and "medical aid in dying".[24] "Every institution must offer end of life care, [including "medical aid in dying", a euphemism for euthanasia] to such persons upon request".[25] Individual doctors, nurses and other medical professionals may for reasons of conscience refuse to participate in administering euthanasia: "A physician may refuse to administer medical aid in dying because of personal convictions, and a health professional may refuse to take part in administering it for the same reason. In such a case, the physician or health care professional must nevertheless ensure that continuity of care is provided for the patient in accordance with their code of ethics and the patient's wishes."[26] A physician with conscientious objections "must, as soon as possible, notify the executive director of the institution …and forward the request form given to the physician, to the executive director… The executive director of the institution or designated person must then take the necessary steps to find, as soon as possible, another physician willing to deal with the request."[27] Many physicians would find it impossible to square this obligation with the clear ethical principle that to provide such a referral is to be complicit in any resultant act of killing. Long-term care institutions and hospitals will not even be permitted

---

24   *Act, see* note 20, Chapter I. (3).
25   *Act, see* note 20, Chap III.8.
26   *Act, see* note 20, Chap. VI.50.
27   *Act, see* note 20, Chap. IV.31.

the minimal rights accorded to doctors and nurses. On the contrary, "every institution must include a clinical program for end-of-life care [including euthanasia] in its organization plan"; and "the plan must be consistent with ministerial policy directions."[28] Even palliative-care hospices "must adopt a code of ethics with respect to the rights of end-of-life patients, and adopt a policy with respect to end-of-life care."[29]

Under the Quebec legislation state policy will be paramount, and will destroy the right of institutions to honour their longstanding ethical principles. Thus for example, a Catholic, or other religiously-based hospital, dedicated to upholding respect for human life – to preserving life rather than destroying it -- will either have to abandon its principles, or be shut down. In effect, Quebec, far from enlarging human freedom will diminish it, by abolishing those institutions that refuse to kill patients under their care.

The Supreme Court's Ruling in Carter v Canada (Attorney General)

The Criminal Code and Gloria Taylor

On February 6th, 2015, the Supreme Court of Canada, speaking as "the Court" to emphasize the weight of its decision, unanimously allowed an appeal from the British Columbia Court of Appeal,[30] thereby setting out conditions under which Sections 14 and 241(b) of

---

28   *Act, see* note 20, Chap III.9.
29   *Act, see* note 20, Chap. III.15.
30   *Carter, see* note 1, para. 128.

the *Criminal Code of Canada* would no longer apply.[31] Section 14 addresses the issue of consent to death, stating that "no person is entitled to consent to have death inflicted on him, and such consent does not affect the criminal responsibility of any person by whom death may be inflicted on the person by whom consent is given."[32] Section 241(b) relates specifically to the topic of assisted suicide, and therefore physician-assisted suicide, stating that "everyone who… (b) aids or abets a person to commit suicide, whether suicide ensues or not, is guilty of an indictable offence and liable to imprisonment for a term not exceeding fourteen years."[33]

In 2010, Kay (Kathleen) Carter died by assisted suicide in Switzerland, accompanied by her daughter Lee Carter and son-in-law, Hollis Johnson. Lee Carter and Hollis Johnson had not been prosecuted for accompanying Kay Carter and assisting in her suicide and they were not charged with any crime. On April 26, 2011, Lee and her husband Hollis launched a lawsuit with the assistance of the BC Civil Liberties Association based on the premise that Kay Carter should not have had to leave the country to commit suicide and that Lee and Hollis should not have had to worry about the law against assisting suicide. On August 15, 2011 The BC Civil Liberties Association added Gloria Taylor as an additional plaintiff via an Amended Notice of Civil Claim. Taylor had been diagnosed with amyotrophic lateral sclerosis (ALS) which causes progressive

---

31   *Criminal Code of Canada*, RSC 1985, c C-46 [*Criminal Code*]. http://laws-lois.justice.gc.ca/eng/acts/C-46/
32   *Criminal Code*, s 14.
33   *Criminal Code*, s 241.

muscle weakness. Taylor was not in the last stages of the disease but her arrival in the case made her the lead plaintiff and allowed trial Justice Lynn Smith to fast track the proceedings.

Together, the claimants argued that the Criminal Code provisions prohibiting assistance in committing suicide (sections 14, 21, 22, 222, and 241) were unconstitutional. They contended that Ms. Taylor should not have to make the "'cruel choice' between killing herself while she was still physically capable of doing so, or giving up the ability to exercise any control over the manner and timing of her death."[34]

At the British Columbia Supreme Court, the trial judge broke with the precedent set in *Rodriguez* by concluding that there is a strong societal consensus in support of physician-assisted dying where that assistance is "clearly consistent with the patient's wishes and best interests, and [provided] in order to relieve suffering."[35] Ultimately the trial judge held, among other things, that society's views on physician-assisted dying have sufficiently developed to warrant a change in the law. In addition, on the basis of evidence presented at trial and in the decision, the trial judge concluded that while no current jurisdiction permitting physician-assisted dying has "achieved perfection," a number of experts and medical professionals believe that these jurisdictions "work well in protecting patients from abuse while allowing competent patients to choose the timing of their deaths."[36] The judge

---

34   *Carter, see* note 1, para. 13.
35   *Carter v Canada*, 2012 BCSC 886, 287 CCC (3d) 1, para 358 [*BCSC*].
36   *Carter, see* note 1, para. 685.

concluded her analysis by declaring the prohibition unconstitutional, granting a one-year suspension of this ruling to allow Parliament time to respond, but providing Gloria Taylor with a personal constitutional exemption protecting from prosecution any doctor who might hasten her death.[37] In the event, Gloria Taylor died of natural causes unrelated to her ALS, and so Canada has yet to see its first case of legal doctor-hastened death.

The British Columbia Court of Appeal overturned the decision of the trial judge. Writing for the 2-1 majority, the Honourable Madam Justice Newbury noted that the law set out in *Rodriguez* was still valid and that the trial judge was bound by this law on the principle of *stare decisis*.[38] This phrase is legal Latin for "let the decision stand", which is the doctrine of binding precedent. The doctrine means that a previous decision of a higher court is authoritative in all future cases in which the facts are substantially the same. However, the Supreme Court of Canada rejected the arguments accepted by the Court of Appeal, and ruled that, as in its 2013 decision in *Canada (Attorney General) v Bedford*,[39] trial courts may reconsider settled rulings "if new legal issues are raised as a consequence of significant developments in the law, or if there is a change in the circumstances or evidence that fundamentally shifts the parameters of the debate."[40] The Supreme Court concluded by allowing the

---

37 *Carter, see* note 1, para. 1414.
38 *Carter v Canada*, 2013 BCCA 435, 51 BCLR (5th) 213.
39 *Canada (Attorney General) v Bedford*, 2013 SCC 72, [2013] 3 SCR 1101 [*Bedford*].
40 *Bedford, see* note 46, para. 42.

appeal to change the law but again suspending its implementation for twelve months.

The Supreme Court's overriding of the will of Parliament

To date there has been little comment on how that decision radically contradicts the expressed will of the elected representatives of the people in Parliament. Ironically the Supreme Court has acknowledged that "high deference"[41] is owed to Parliament on this issue, while at the same time demonstrating disregard of Parliament's oft-expressed will. This will has been expressed repeatedly since 1991 by its rejection of no fewer than fifteen initiatives in the House of Commons and the Senate to legalize euthanasia and assisted suicide.[42] Of the fifteen, six were private members' bills from both ends of the political spectrum seeking to decriminalize assisted suicide.[43] In 2014 alone, two bills concerning both "passive" and "active" euthanasia were tabled by Members of Parliament, subject to further review.[44] Despite all these efforts to pass legislation in favour of euthanasia and assisted suicide, Parliament has repeatedly refused to alter the Criminal Code's prohibition of euthanasia and assisted suicide.

---

41   *Carter, see* note 1, p. 62

42   Aaron Wherry, "Assisted Suicide: What Will Parliament Do Now?" *Macleans* (February 6, 2015); http://www.macleans.ca/politics/assisted-suicide-what-will-parliament-do-now/

43   *Carter, see* note 1, para 6.

44   Parliament of Canada, "Private Member's Bill, 41st Parliament, 2nd Session, C-582" http://www.parl.gc.ca/LEGISInfo/BillDetails.aspx?Language=E&Mode=1&billId=6477700; Parliament of Canada, "Private Member's Bill, 41st Parliament, 2nd Session, C-581" http://www.parl.gc.ca/LEGISInfo/BillDetails.aspx?Language=E&Mode=1&billId=6477659

The most recent bill to come to a vote in the House of Commons, was rejected by a crushing majority of 228 to 59.[45] A majority of MPs in every party except the Bloc Québecois voted against the bill.

An Expert Panel post-Carter

In spite of the clear position repeatedly taken by the Parliament of Canada, the Province of Quebec, as we have seen, passed Bill 52 legalizing medically-assisted dying.[46] Moreover, the federal government has been given until February 2016 to enact legislation that conforms to the Court's ruling in *Carter*.[47] On July 17th, 2015 the then Minister of Justice and Attorney General of Canada Peter MacKay, and Minister of Health Rona Ambrose announced the appointment of a three-member Expert Panel to consult with Canadians on how to respond to the Supreme Court's decision in *Carter*. As noted in the Introduction, the panel includes: Chairman, Harvey Max Chochinov, MD, PhD, FRCPC, Distinguished Professor of Psychiatry and Canada Research Chair in Palliative Care at the University of Manitoba and Director of the Manitoba Palliative Care Research Unit, CancerCare Manitoba; Catherine Frazee, D.Litt., LL.D., Professor Emerita at Ryerson University, where, prior to her retirement in 2010, she served as Professor of Distinction and Co-Director of the Ryerson-RBC Institute for Disability Studies

---

45   Parliament of Canada, "Private Member's Bill, 40th Parliament, 3rd Session, C-384" http://www.parl.gc.ca/LegisInfo/BillDetails.aspx?Language=E&Mode=1&billId=4328668

46   National Assembly, *Bill 52: An Act Respecting End-of-Life Care* (2014), http://www.dyingwithdignity.ca/database/files/library/final_of_quebec_bill.pdf

47   *Carter, see* note 1, para. 128.

Research and Education; and Benoît Pelletier, LL.B., LL.M., LL.D., LL.D., Professor of Law, University of Ottawa, constitutional expert and former member of the National Assembly of Quebec from 1998 to 2008, and Quebec Cabinet minister from 2003 to 2008. The panel is expected to issue its report after the federal election in late 2015.[48]

The Supreme Court's "Test" for new legislation

In arriving at its decision, the Supreme Court narrowed its analysis to sections 14 and 241(b) of the *Criminal Code* as being "at the core of the constitutional challenge," stating that the remaining provisions "are engaged [only] so long as the provision of assistance in dying is itself an 'unlawful act' or offence."[49]

Prohibiting assisted suicide violates your "right to life"

The Supreme Court found that the *Criminal Code* provisions unjustifiably infringe all the rights articulated in Section 7 of the *Charter of Rights and Freedoms*. That Section states that "everyone has the right to life, liberty and security of the person and the right not to be deprived thereof except in accordance with the principles of fundamental justice."[50] While the Court had held previously In Rodriguez that section 241(b) of the Criminal Code *did* infringe the *right*

---

48   Government of Canada. "Government of Canada Establishes External Panel on options for a legislative response to *Carter v. Canada*." *News Release* (17 July, 2015) http://news.gc.ca/web/article-en. do?nid=1002949

49   *Carter, see* note 1, para 20.

50   *Canadian Charter of Rights and Freedoms,* Part I of the Constitution Act, 1982, being Schedule B to the Canada Act 1982 (UK), 1982, c 11, s 7.

to security of the person in section 7; nevertheless, this infringement was "in accordance with the principles of fundamental justice", and therefore justified.[51] The Court in *Carter* found that this same provision unjustifiably violated the *right to life* of the patient.

Who is eligible for assisted suicide, and under what circumstances?

In effect, the Court held that sections 14 and 241(b) of the Criminal Code were void insofar as they deprived

> a *competent* adult of such assistance where (1) the person affected *clearly consents* to the termination of life; and (2) the person had *a grievous and irremediable medical condition* (including an illness, disease or disability) that *causes enduring suffering that is intolerable to the individual* in the circumstances of his or her condition.[52]

Put simply, the test laid out by the Supreme Court comprises: 1) the kind of persons eligible for physician-assisted suicide; 2) the nature of the request that is required; and 3) the kinds of circumstances eligible persons must find themselves in to have their request be considered.

The second part of the Supreme Court's test has its foundations in a large body of jurisprudence protecting patient autonomy in medical decision-making. The recent Supreme Court case, *AC v Manitoba (Director of Child and Family Services)*,

---

51 [1993] 3 SCR 519 Rodriguez v British Columbia (Attorney General).
52 *Carter*, see note 1, para. 4 [Emphasis added].

endorses the "tenacious relevance in our legal system of the principle that competent individuals are – and should be – free to make decisions about their bodily integrity."[53] As noted in *Fleming v Reid* by the Ontario Court of Appeal, the right to make determinations about one's medical state "is not vitiated by the fact that serious risks or consequences, including death, may flow from the patient's decision."[54] This right of medical self-determination has always included the right of competent adults to refuse or request withdrawal of medical treatment for themselves, with very few exceptions, such as when public health is threatened. The Court used this fact to make an analogy to the right to request euthanasia or physician-assisted suicide, finding that both refusals of treatment and euthanasia or physician-assisted suicide result in death, and claiming that there is no ethically or legally valid distinction between the common-law right to refuse treatment, which is seen as valid and legal, and the right to be killed with medical assistance, which should therefore also be seen as valid and legal.

The third part of the test is grounded in the language first proposed by the plaintiffs before the British Columbia Supreme Court. In their court action, Ms. Taylor and others argued that:

> 1. A person is "grievously and irremediably ill" when he or she has a serious medical condition that has been diagnosed as such by a medical practitioner and which:

---

53   *AC v Manitoba (Director of Child and Family Services)*, 2009 SCC 30, [2009] 2 SCR 181, para 39 [*Manitoba*].

54   *Carter, see* note 1, para. 67; see also *Fleming v Reid*, 4 OR (3d) 74 (CA).

a) is without remedy, as determined by reference to treatment options acceptable to the person; and

b) causes the person enduring physical, psychological or psychosocial suffering that:

i) is intolerable to that person; and

ii) cannot be alleviated by any medical treatment acceptable to that person.

2. A "medical condition" means an illness, disease or disability, and includes a disability arising from traumatic injury.[55]

Despite this broad and subjective definition of "grievously and irremediably ill" having been repeated by the Court of Appeal in its judgment, the Supreme Court made no such reference to the list of conditions put forward by the plaintiffs. With the exception of a brief note on the term "irremediable" (see discussion below), the Supreme Court only used the terms "grievous and irremediable" in describing the third component of its test.

Outstanding Questions

a) The vexed issue of competency

The test outlined by the Supreme Court leaves a number of questions not fully answered, for example the issue of "competency". While the basic definition of a "competent adult" may be generally assumed, a

---

55   *BCSC, see* note 35, para. 24.

glance at comparable jurisprudence suggests that this may not be the case. In fact, in situations involving informed consent or cases dealing with the competency of elderly persons when making decisions about the distribution of their estate, definitions of "competency" are frequently contested.[56] By the same token, when a patient is facing a "grievous and irremediable medical condition," what is the limit of his or her competency? When a medical condition disrupts a patient's cognitive capacities or even disproportionately accelerates a patient's perceptions about the extent of their suffering (for example, in cases of clinical depression), should that patient be classified as "competent"? Neither the trial judge in her initial framing of the test nor the Supreme Court suggests ways to deal with these crucial questions.

In its ruling the Supreme Court concluded that "concerns about decisional capacity and vulnerability arise in all end-of-life medical decisions," and that "it is possible for physicians, with due care and attention to the seriousness of the decision involved, to adequately assess decisional capacity."[57] Despite the Court's finding that a regime which permits physician-assisted suicide can safely exist by granting physicians the discretionary authority to determine competency, the decision fails to offer specific guidelines upon which this discretionary authority ought to be based.

b) What is "a grievous and irremediable medical condition"?

The issue of competency is also tied to the question of

---

56   See for example *Scott v Cousins* (2001), 37 ETR (2d) 113 (Ont SCJ).

57   *Carter, see* note 1, paras. 115-16.

suffering, since a patient's capacity to make informed decisions about end-of-life care is inevitably viewed in the light of the medical circumstances in which they find themself. If a patient is "competent, fully-informed, and free from coercion or duress,"[58] as the trial judge accepted Ms. Taylor to be, then that patient must also have "a grievous and irremediable medical condition (including an illness, disease or disability) that causes enduring suffering that is intolerable to the individual."[59] What constitutes a grievous and irremediable medical condition?

In its test, the Court noted that "a grievous and irremediable condition" includes (though is not necessarily limited to) "an illness, disease or disability."[60] This may suggest that there are other types of conditions available to patients seeking physician-assisted suicide. In its clarification of the term "irremediable," the Court specifically noted that the term "does not require the patient to undertake treatments that are not acceptable to the individual."[61] In effect, an "irremediable" disease need not necessarily be defined as an illness that is impossible to cure, but one which is impossible to cure if no further interventions are taken (however invasive or non-invasive they may be). Arguably, this distinction could have the effect of lowering the required threshold for the kinds of conditions acceptable under the Court's framework for tolerating physician-assisted suicide.

---

58   *BCSC, see* note 35, para. 1243.
59   *Carter, see* note 1, para. 4.
60   *Carter, see* note 1, para 4.
61   *Carter, see* note 1, para. 127.

c) What is "enduring and intolerable suffering"?

The limiting condition in the Court's assessment for determining whether a medical condition is "grievous and irremediable" is its requirement that the condition cause "enduring suffering that is intolerable to the individual in the circumstances of his or her condition."[62] On this basis, the Supreme Court seems to follow the approach taken both by the trial judge and the Supreme Court in AC. In the latter case Justice Binnie noted that a person's choice to reject potentially life-saving treatment is surely done "out of a deeply personal and fundamental belief about how they wish to live, or cease to live..."[63] As the Supreme Court elaborated in *Carter*, physician-assisted suicide "represents [a] deeply personal response to serious pain and suffering."[64] In reflecting upon this measure for assessing a patient's degree of suffering, one finds that on its face the test is largely subjective. While the Court expressed its confidence that a doctor will use his or her discretion responsibly to diagnose an individual patient's condition, the language of the test seems to suggest that the discretion, and therefore the decision, ultimately rests with the patient.

d) How can we be sure that someone has actually consented to be killed?

The issue of "clear consent" is also critically important. In its ruling the Supreme Court confidently dismissed

---

62   *Carter, see* note 1, para. 4.
63   *Manitoba, see* note 53, para. 219.
64   *Carter, see* note 1, para. 68.

concerns that a regime permitting physician-assisted suicide could lead to problems related to knowing what the patient really wants. Ms. Taylor's choice to end her life was described as "competent, fully-informed, and free from coercion or duress."[65] All the evidence that countries like the Netherlands and Belgium have fallen into an overly-permissive assisted-dying regime was rejected. Arguments suggesting "that a slippery slope is at work" were dismissed on the ground that "the permissive regime in Belgium is the product of a very different medico-legal culture"[66] where assisted dying was "already prevalent and embedded in the medical culture"[67] prior to legalization.

Notwithstanding the rulings made by the Supreme Court, there still remain unanswered questions about the issue of consent. While the Court suggested that decisions about assisted dying will be consistently "competent, fully-informed, and free from coercion or duress," as they were for Ms. Taylor, it did not address the possible barriers to free consent that often arise from the (sometimes subtle) social, cultural, and economic pressures present in a given society. It is to these additional and less obvious barriers that we now turn.

e) Protections for Patients

Among the many questions left unanswered by the Supreme Court decision in *Carter*, one of the most important is the protections available for patients. In the adjudicative facts described by the British

---

65   *BCSC, see* note 35, para. 1243
66   *Carter, see* note 1, para. 112.
67   *BCSC, see* note 35, para. 660.

Columbia Supreme Court, Justice Smith addressed the potential impacts on palliative care for patients once new legislation permitting physician-assisted suicide has been enacted. She considered evidence from a range of medical experts and determined that a regime permitting physician-assisted suicide could safely exist, after rejecting the testimony of witnesses like Dr. Herbert Hendin, internationally renowned for his research in suicide prevention.[68] We are less sanguine than Justice Smith about the prospects of abuse in light of the State of Oregon's recent experience.

f) Burdening Loved Ones

Oregon was the first American state to legalize physician-assisted suicide. Implemented in 1997 following a three-year injunction while it was being challenged,[69] Oregon's *Death With Dignity Act* (DWDA) "allows terminally-ill adult Oregonians to obtain and use prescriptions from their physicians for self-administered, lethal doses of medications."[70] Over the next eighteen years Oregon saw a steady increase of DWDA deaths and prescription recipients, recording an all-time high number of prescriptions and deaths in 2014.[71] In the list of end-of-life concerns compiled in the Death with Dignity Annual Reports since the law's enactment, an average of 40 per

---

68   *BCSC, see* note 35, para. 847.

69   Oregon Health Authority, *The Oregon Death With Dignity Act – Oregon Revised Statutes.* https://public.health.oregon.gov/ ProviderPartnerResources/EvaluationResearch/DeathwithDignityAct/ Pages/ors.aspx

70   Oregon Public Health Division, *Oregon's Death with Dignity Act Report, 2014*, p. 1; https://public.health.oregon.gov/ ProviderPartnerResources/EvaluationResearch/DeathwithDignityAct/ Documents/year17.pdf

71   Oregon Public Health Division, DWDA Report, *see* note 70, p. 1.

cent of DWDA prescription recipients expressed the wish *not to be a burden on their family, friends, and caregivers* as one reason for seeking Oregon's assisted-dying services.[72]

The concern about burdening loved ones, whether family members or general caregivers, has also been widely reported in the State of Washington. Washington passed its *Death with Dignity Act* in 2008,[73] allowing "terminally ill adults seeking to end their lives in a humane and dignified manner [and] to request lethal doses of medication from medical and osteopathic physicians"[74] According to the Washington State Department of Health 2014 Death with Dignity Act Report, being a burden on family, friends, and caregivers was an end-of-life concern shared by 59 per cent of participants .[75] This figure has increased significantly from 2009, the first year the law came into effect, when only 23 per cent of participants reported concerns about being burdens to their loved ones.[76] Like the State of Oregon, Washington has also witnessed a steady rise in the number of recipients of assisted suicide in each successive year since the law's enactment.[77]

---

72   Oregon Public Health Division, DWDA Report, *see* note 70, p. 5 [emphasis added]. This percentage is the same for 2014 recipients as well the average recorded from 1997-2013.

73   Washington State Department of Health, *Death With Dignity Act. Initiative Measure No. 1000.* http://www.wsha.org/files/i1000%20text.pdf

74   Washington State Department of Health 2014 Death with Dignity Act Report, p. 1. http://www.doh.wa.gov/portals/1/Documents/Pubs/422-109-DeathWithDignityAct2014.pdf

75   Washington, 2014 DWDA Report, *see* note 74, p. 7.

76   Washington State Department of Health, 2009 Death With Dignity Act Report, p. 7. http://www.doh.wa.gov/portals/1/Documents/5300/DWDA2009.pdf

77   Washington State Department of Health, 2013 Death With Dignity Act Report, p. 4. http://www.doh.wa.gov/portals/1/Documents/Pubs/422-109-DeathWithDignityAct2013.pdf

Another barrier to genuine consent can be economic. Some patients have been pointed towards assisted suicide because the medications prescribed by their physicians were deemed too expensive. We present an expanded discussion of these issues in Chapter Three.

Conclusion

On February 6th, 2015, in the Carter case, the Supreme Court of Canada announced an extraordinary new reading of the Charter of Rights and Freedoms. The rights to life, liberty and security of the person guaranteed by Section 7 were now found to be breached by an absolute prohibition on physician-assisted suicide and euthanasia In effect, these rights were interpreted by the Court to include the right to be killed with medical assistance. The centuries-old prohibition on assisting another person to commit suicide, or consenting to another person assisting one to commit suicide or giving one a lethal injection was now pronounced a violation of the rights to life, liberty and security of the person . In self-justification the Supreme Court alluded to the steady shift in public opinion towards support for physician-assisted suicide. Ironically, it completely ignored the will of the people's elected representatives in Parliament, as well as many expert professional bodies, both in Canada and other countries, who over the past twenty years and more have continued to support the legal prohibition of assisted suicide. Is it not strange that the nine unelected judges of our highest court are evidently more swayed by current public opinion than our elected Members of Parliament? It is just as strange that nine judges, without a murmur of dissent, could concur with the reasoning required to find a right to state-approved self-destruction in the Charter right to life. It remains to be seen how much Parliament will be able to salvage from the wreckage of the Supreme Court decision.

Chapter 3 *

The State of the Law throughout the World

Culturally and ethically Canada has never been "an island unto itself". We have always been influenced by the United States, Europe, and to a lesser extent, the world. Many people have the impression that euthanasia and assisted suicide are topics of hot controversy everywhere. This is far from being the case. The practice continues to be illegal in Asia, Africa, Latin America (except for Colombia), most of Europe, and most states in the U.S. A handful of countries have recently had intense, thoughtful discussions of the issue. We'll start by reviewing those discussions.

Germany

Current legislation governing end-of-life care expresses a keen determination to protect life. This reflects a conscious repudiation of Germany's past identification with euthanasia and eugenics policies. After the rise of the Third Reich in the 1930s, the Nazi government legislated compulsory euthanasia for disabled children. The regime planned to extend this policy to all "useless eaters" but popular opposition, spearheaded by the German Catholic bishops forced it to drop the euthanasia program until the holocaust began.   At the time, Hitler was furious with the church for compelling him to back down, and vowed to punish it after the war was over.[1]

** Chapter 3 written with the assistance of Julia Giancola.*
1   Dowbiggin, I, A Concise History of Euthanasia: Life, Death, God, and Medicine. (Lanham, Md.: Rowman & Littlefield, 2005), p. 111.

After the 1960s the notion of euthanasia as essentially a passive, patient-centered practice gained traction apparently thanks to dramatic changes in demography (an aging population), and medical technology.[2] Since that time death has become a major topic of public discussion.

During the 1960s and 1970s German public opinion on euthanasia underwent a pronounced shift. This was in part because American and British Euthanasia organizations began to revive the early twentieth-century, pre-Nazi view of assisted suicide. These organizations were helped in their efforts to gain acceptability by abandoning the old language of mercy killing with its menacing overtones. In its place they adopted more soothing diction, eliminating any reference to killing in favour of phrases such as the "right to die" or "dying with dignity," or "assistance in dying".[3] In 1974, Abigail Van Buren of the Euthanasia Society of America, publicly admitted that "a bill with the word 'euthanasia' in it will never get passed".[4] By these strategies pro-euthanasia groups were able to transform people's attitudes towards euthanasia. Their influence extended to Canada, Britain and Germany, among other countries.

German Medical Association: the physician's duty is to restore life

In February 2011 the German Medical Association published a revision of its Principles regarding the

---

2   Dowbiggin, *Concise History of Euthanasia*, p. 111.
3   Dowbiggin, *Concise History of Euthanasia*, p. 124.
4   Dowbiggin, '*Concise History of Euthanasia*, p. 124.

accompaniment of the dying process by physicians.[5] According to the new preamble "it is the duty of the physician to protect and restore the patient's health as well as to alleviate the patient's suffering and assist dying patients until death, while preserving life according to the patient's right of self-determination".[6] The revised Principles also state, "The physician's involvement in suicide is not a medical task." There is thus no doubt that from both a legal and a medical perspective, the German Medical Association does not consider assisted suicide to belong within the definition of medical care. It is emphatic that the physician's duty is to preserve rather than end life. [7]

In addition, in December 2014, the German Ethics Council stated that the law should not be changed to permit assisted suicide.[8] Both the German Ethics Council and the Federal Medical Council (Bundesärztekammer) agreed that doctors should not routinely be asked to help patients commit suicide.[9] However, both organizations agreed that "in 'exceptional circumstances', decisions of conscience by a doctor in the context of a "trusting doctor-patient

---

5 German Reference Centre for Ethics in the Life Sciences (DRZE): German Medical Association, *Principles regarding the accompaniment of the dying process by physicians*. Retrieved June 17 2015 http://www.drze.de/in-focus/euthanasia/legal-regulations

6 German Medical Association, *Principles regarding the accompaniment of the dying process*.

7 German Medical Association, *Principles regarding the accompaniment of the dying process*.

8 "Ethics Council Rejects Assisted Suicide Law". *The Local* (December 19, 2014). Retrieved June 22 2015 http://www.thelocal. de/20141219/ethics-council-rejects-assisted-suicide-terminal-illness-dying-law-bill

9 "Ethics Council Rejects Assisted Suicide Law".

relationship" should be respected".[10]   Dr. Carola Reimann, deputy chairman of the Social Democratic Party parliamentary group, and Peter Hintze, Vice-President of the German Parliament, put forward a bill to legalize the practice of assisted suicide. They claimed that the bill was aimed at giving doctors more certainty about the possible legal consequences of helping a patient to end their life. In response, the President of the German Foundation for Patient Protection declared that "The MPs are twisting the recommendations of the Ethics Council in their favour".[11] Palliative Foundation spokesman Thomas Sitte endorsed this criticism, bluntly stating that "dying cannot be normalized. We doctors have a special duty and responsibility for life".[12]

Assisted suicide remains illegal in Germany

> Section 216 of the German Criminal Code reads:

> (1) If a person is induced to kill by the express and earnest request of the victim the penalty shall be imprisonment from six months to five years. [13]

In German law, suicide by itself is not a criminal act.[14] However, "suicide is [still] regarded as unethical and

---

10   "Ethics Council Rejects Assisted Suicide Law".
11   "Ethics Council Rejects Assisted Suicide Law".
12   "Ethics Council Rejects Assisted Suicide Law".
13   German Criminal Code, Section 216, translated by Michael Bohlander (2015).
14   German Reference Centre for Ethics in the Life Sciences (DRZE), 'The Situation in the Federal Republic of Germany'. Retrieved June 17 2015 http://www.drze.de/in-focus/euthanasia/legal-regulations

something that should be condemned."[15] In practice the law on assisted suicide is complex. If assistance in committing suicide is given by a physician or close relative, the patient's expressed wish to die is critically important. Failing to document the patient's wish for suicide renders the act a criminal offence[16]. Even when it is done at the patient's request it can still be a punishable offence.[17]

Australia

Australia provides an instructive example of the intensity of the euthanasia debate. It is the only country where previously introduced legislation permitting euthanasia in one jurisdiction was later struck down by a higher jurisdiction. What is the historical trajectory of assisted suicide and euthanasia in Australia?

In 1995, the Northern Territory Parliament passed the Rights of The Terminally Ill Act. The Act gave terminally-ill individuals the right to receive assistance from a medically-qualified person to terminate their life in a humane manner.[18] Even though the act was passed, it ran into fierce opposition. The Australian Medical Association denounced the law, and urged that more resources be invested in palliative care for the terminally ill. Anti-euthanasia organizations

---

15   Gabriele Wolfslast, "Physician-assisted suicide and the German criminal law", in Dieter Birnbacher and Edgar Dahl (eds.), *Giving Death a Helping Hand: Physician-Assisted Suicide and Public Policy. An International Perspective*. New York: Springer, 2008, p. 94.

16   'The Situation in the Federal Republic of Germany'.

17   Gabriele Wolfslast, "Physician-assisted suicide and the German criminal law", p. 93.

18   Original legislation permitting euthanasia in 1995: http://www.nt.gov.au/lant/parliamentary-business/committees/rotti/rotti95.pdf

campaigned to overturn the law. Church leaders also expressed dissatisfaction with the law, fearing that the implicit devaluing of life would jeopardize patient-physician trust.[19]

The Australian Parliament prohibits assisted suicide in all its territories

In 1997, the House of Representatives and Senate of the Commonwealth of Australia adopted a new Euthanasia Law prohibiting all regions under its jurisdiction from legalizing assisted suicide or euthanasia. This effectively prevented territories from legalizing euthanasia on their own. The new amended law applied to the Northern Territory (Self-Government) Act of 1978, Capital Territory (Self-Government) Act of 1988, and the Norfolk Island Act of 1979.[20] In other words the national Australian Parliament strictly prohibits euthanasia in all of its three territories. This is a direct consequence of the Northern Territory's Rights of The Terminally Ill Act.

Assisted suicide remains illegal in the six self-governing states

Yet in the matter of euthanasia and assisted suicide the national parliament does not have jurisdiction over the six self-governing states—Queensland, Western Australia, South Australia, New South Wales, Victoria and the island

---

19   E. Blacksher. "Euthanasia in Australia. *The Hastings Center Report*, 25(5)' (1995), p. 47. Retrieved from http://search.proquest.com/docview/222378814?accountid=14771

20   Original legislation permitting euthanasia in 1995: http://www.nt.gov.au/lant/parliamentary-business/committees/rotti/rotti95.pdf

of Tasmania. Euthanasia recently came very close to being legalized in Tasmania. In 2013, a private member's bill, put forward by Labour Premier Lara Giddings and Greens leader Nick McKim, was narrowly defeated by a vote of thirteen to eleven.[21] Despite relentless pressure from the euthanasia lobby, buttressed by significant public support for physician-assisted suicide, the elected MPs demonstrated their profound respect for the existing law by defying public opinion. Those who opposed the bill were strengthened in their conviction by a Law Society report that "found flaws in the Bill's drafting, and questioned whether it could protect vulnerable patients."[22] Despite the state of public opinion, which has been so influential with Canadian jurists, the majority of the Tasmanian Parliament showed themselves to be resolute in protecting the lives of the vulnerable.

France

At the time of writing, euthanasia and assisted suicide are against the law in France.[23] However, recent promises by President François Hollande to revisit the issue have led to passionate public debate. Hollande vowed to review the concept of "right to die with dignity".[24]

On April 22nd, 2005 France passed The Rights of Patients

---

21   "David Beniuk. Tasmania's Euthanasia Bill fails. News (Oct.17, 2013). Retrieved from http://www.news.com.au/national/breaking-news/tasmanias-euthanasia-bill-fails-narrowly/story-e6frfku9-1226741999723

22   Beniuk, Tasmania's Euthanasia Bill fails.

23   Guardian Staff. "Euthanasia and assisted suicide laws around the world". The *Guardian* (July 17, 2014). Accessed June 9th from http://www.theguardian.com/society/2014/jul/17/euthanasia-assisted-suicide-laws-world

24   "Euthanasia and assisted suicide laws around the world".

and End of Life Act. According to a *Guardian* report, "this law allowed doctors to decide to 'limit or stop any treatment that is not useful, is disproportionate or has no other object than to artificially prolong life", and to use pain-killing drugs that might "as a side effect, shorten life."[25]

Article 1 of the Act states:

> These acts [extraordinary medical measures] should not be pursued by an unreasonable obstinacy. When they appear useless, disproportionate or having no effect as the only artificial maintenance of life, they can be suspended or not be undertaken. In this case, the doctor safeguarding the dignity of the dying and ensures the quality of life by providing care referred to in Article L. 1110-10.[26]

In sum, the law does not in any way legalize euthanasia or assisted suicide. It only authorizes the withdrawal of medical treatment when its continuance would amount to "unreasonable obstinacy", or would appear to be "needless, disproportionate or having the sole effect of artificially maintaining life".[27] As is well known, this has been good medical practice for a very long time, and patients have always had the right to order the cessation of medical treatment. Yet it is

---

25   "Euthanasia and assisted suicide laws around the world".

26   A. Baumann, G. Audibert, F. Claudot, L. Puybasset. "Ethics review: End of life legislation - the French model". *Critical Care* 2009; 13(1): p. 204. doi:10.1186/cc7148

27   B. Clin, O. Ferrant (2010). "Law of 22 April 2005 on patients' rights and the end of life in France: Setting the boundaries of euthanasia, with regard to current legislation in other European countries." *Medicine, Science and the Law* 2010 Oct; 50(4): pp. 183-8.

reported that the new law has caused much confusion among the general public, doctors, and patients.[28] This confusion has contributed to the current impassioned debate on end-of-life care in France. It has to be stressed that the refusal or cessation of medical treatment at the patient's request can in no way be defined as euthanasia, and is in every country a patient's right. [29]

On March 11th, 2015 the French National Assembly debated a private member's bill creating new rights for patients and people nearing the end of life.[30] The bill would allow terminally ill patients to refuse further treatment and enter a "deep sleep" through sedation until they die. If the sedation is not clinically indicated to relieve suffering, in effect it constitutes "slow euthanasia". The law would also allow individuals to make legally binding declarations, or "living wills", stating that they do not want to be kept alive artificially if they are too ill to decide.[31] Again, it must be stressed that the bill does not make euthanasia or assisted suicide legal. Yet it has provoked much public debate. The French Senate is expected to debate the bill later this year (2015).

---

28   Government of France. End-of-life Debate. (March 10, 2015). Retrieved July 11, 2015 from http://www.gouvernement.fr/en/end-of-life-debate

29   *World Medical Ethics Manual,* 2nd edition (2009). Chapter Two, p. 44. Retrieved from http://www.wma.net/en/30publications/30ethicsmanual/pdf/chap_2_en.pdf

30   Government of France. End-of-life Debate. (March 10, 2015). Retrieved July 11, 2015 from http://www.gouvernement.fr/en/end-of-life-debate

31   Angelique Chrisafis. "French parliament votes through 'deep sleep' law for terminally ill". *Guardian* (March 17, 2015) http://www.theguardian.com/world/2015/mar/17/french-parliament-deep-sleep-law-terminally-ill-euthanasia

British House of Lords

The House of Lords of Great Britain and Northern Ireland (the U.K.) has addressed the issue of euthanasia in depth more than once. Each time it has voted to uphold the existing law against euthanasia and assisted suicide. The first debate was in 2004, when Lord Joffe introduced the Assisted Dying for the Terminally Ill Bill. Under its terms, "only people with less than six months to live, who were suffering unbearably and deemed to be of sound mind and not depressed would be able to end their life."[32] The bill generated much controversy. In an open letter to the Members of both Houses of Parliament, the leaders Britain's religious communities wrote, "Assisted suicide and euthanasia will radically change the social air we all breathe by severely undermining respect for life. The previous Lords' Committee on this issue opposed assisted dying because of concern that 'vulnerable people - the elderly, lonely, sick or distressed - would feel pressure, whether real or imagined, to request early death. This concern is just as valid today. The so-called 'right to die' would inexorably become the duty to die and potentially economic pressures and convenience would come to dominate decision-making."[33] This eloquent statement inspired the opponents of the bill to demonstrate outside Parliament and to submit a petition with 100,000 signatures to the Prime Minister

---

32   Assisted-dying legislation in the UK. BBC Ethics Guide (2014). Retrieved from (http://www.bbc.co.uk/ethics/euthanasia/overview/asstdyingbill_1.shtml

33   An open letter to all Members of Parliament and of the House of Lords, from leaders of British faith communities of Buddhists, Christians, Hindus, Jews, Muslims and Sikhs, expressing grave concern at continuing and renewed eff orts to legalise euthanasia – (2005)

at his residence in 10 Downing Street.[34]

Baroness Campbell's impassioned appeal

In 2009, during the passage of the Coroners and Justice Act, two amendments were moved to revise the law on assisted suicide to allow it. Neither succeeded.[35] Baroness Campbell, a leading campaigner for disabled people's rights who herself lives with a degenerative condition (spinal muscular atrophy), spoke strongly against the amendment:

> If these amendments were to succeed, despair would be endorsed as a reasonable expectation for which early state-sanctioned death is an effective remedy. Is this really the message that we wish to give disabled and terminally ill people? Is this really the future that we wish to offer those who become terminally ill? Those of us who know what it is to live with a terminal condition are fearful that the tide has already turned against us. If I should ever seek death -- there have been times when my progressive condition challenges me -- I want a guarantee that you are there supporting my continued life and its value. The last thing that I want is for you to give up on me, especially when I need you most. I urge your Lordships to reassure us by

---

34   Assisted-dying legislation in the UK. BBC Ethics Guide (2014). Retrieved from (http://www.bbc.co.uk/ethics/euthanasia/overview/asstdyingbill_1.shtml

35   S. Lipscombe, S.Barber. Assisted Suicide. *Library House of Commons*. (2014, Aug 20).

rejecting this amendment.[36]

The Assisted Dying Bill rejected

The Lords began debating the Assisted Dying Bill, introduced by Lord Falconer, in May 2013. It did not advance beyond First Reading in the 2013-14 session, but was reintroduced in the 2014-15 session. The Bill would have allowed competent adults who are terminally ill to receive assistance in ending their life.[37] The leaders of the major faith communities in Britain issued a joint statement opposing the Bill, arguing that it will "only add to the pressures that many vulnerable, terminally ill people will feel, placing them at increased risk of distress and coercion at a time when they most require love and support".[38] Not Dead Yet UK, a network of disabled people opposed to assisted dying, has commented, "we believe that the campaign to legalise assisted suicide reinforces deep-seated beliefs that the lives of sick and disabled people are not worth as much as other people's. That if you are disabled or terminally ill, it's not worth being alive."[39]

Prime Minister Cameron's opposition to legalization

The assisted dying bill was again debated in July 2014. By the end of an emotionally exhausting ten hours, 65 peers had spoken in favour of the legislation and 62

---

36   Lords Hansard. (July 7, 2009). Column 614 . Retrieved from http://www.publications.parliament.uk/pa/ld200809/ldhansrd/text/90707-0008.htm#09070778000031

37   Lipscombe, Barber. *Assisted Suicide.*

38   Lipscombe, Barber. *Assisted Suicide.*

39   Lipscombe , Barber. *Assisted Suicide.*

against.[40] There was no consensus among any of the professions, -- doctors, senior lawyers, police chiefs, politicians and members of the clergy spoke on both sides. Yet over a period of many years, The House of Lords in Britain has shown itself notably reluctant to pass any bill sanctioning euthanasia or assisted suicide. The House of Commons for the most part has been content to let the Lords take the lead on this issue, although Prime Minister David Cameron recently reaffirmed emphatically his opposition to legalization because of the danger it would pose to the frail and vulnerable.[41] But in the end the House of Commons took the bull by the horns and on 11 September 2015 massively defeated the bill for assisted dying by a margin of 330 to 112.[42] The issue will not likely be raised again for some time in Britain.

Other Countries

A total of 192 countries have laws against euthanasia and physician-assisted suicide. They include the whole of Asia and Africa, the whole of Latin America except Colombia, and all of the Europe with the exception of the Netherlands (2001), Belgium (2002), Albania (1999), and Luxembourg (2008). It was legalized in Colombia by Supreme Court decision in 1997, by Canada by Supreme

---

40   Rowena Mason. "House of Lords Debate Evenly Split Over Assisted Dying Legislation". *Guardian* (July 18, 2014) Retrieved from http://www.theguardian.com/society/2014/jul/18/assisted-dying-legalisation-debate-house-lords

41   https://www.youtube.com/watch?v=u8h_G3K-0vs "PM David Cameron reaffirms opposition to assisted suicide and euthanasia" (June 23, 2015).

42   *Guardian* online, 15 Sept. 2015. http://www.theguardian.com/politics/blog/live/2015/sep/11/mps-debate-and-vote-on-the-assisted-dying-bill-politics-live#block-55f2cdece4b0f3f3043af614

Court decision in 2015, and, in the U.S., in Oregon (1997), Washington (2008), Montana (ambiguously by court decision in 2009) and Vermont (2012).

World Medical Association condemns assisted suicide

A recent statement by the World Medical Association eloquently expresses what amounts to a near global consensus:

> Physicians-assisted suicide, like euthanasia, is unethical and must be condemned by the medical profession. Where the assistance of the physician is intentionally and deliberately directed at enabling an individual to end his or her own life, the physician acts unethically. However the right to decline medical treatment is a basic right of the patient and the physician does not act unethically even if respecting such a wish results in the death of the patient.[43]

Where are Euthanasia and Assisted Suicide Legal?

Out of 196 countries, as of June 2015 euthanasia and assisted suicide are only legal in the Netherlands, Belgium, Colombia, and Luxembourg. Euthanasia is defined by the direct killing of a person, by action or omission. Physician-assisted suicide refers to doctors (or sometimes in practice, nurses) providing the means

---

43   World Medical Association Resolution on Euthanasia, adopted in 2005, and reaffirmed in 2013. http://www.wma.net/en/30publications/10policies/e13b/

for death, most often with a lethal prescription.[44] This means that globally, barely two per cent of countries or jurisdictions legally sanction assisting patients to die.

The Netherlands

In April 2001 the Dutch Euthanasia law was passed, making the Netherlands the first country to legalize euthanasia and assisted suicide.[45] In the Netherlands, euthanasia is legal with consent of the patient, and guidelines have been adopted to allow the killing of newborns with disabilities.[46]

Under the law's requirements of due care, the physician must:

    a) hold the conviction that the request by the patient was voluntary and well considered,

    b) hold the conviction that the patient's suffering was lasting and unbearable,

    c) have informed the patient about the situation he was in and about his prospects,

and the patient must:

    d) hold the conviction that there was no other

---

44   "Is physician-assisted suicide the same as euthanasia?" *World Federation of Right to Die Societies*. Retrieved on July 5th 2015 from http:// www.worldrtd.net/qanda/physician-assisted-suicide-same-euthanasia

45   "Netherlands, first country to legalize euthanasia". *Bulletin of the World Health Organization* (2001) p.79. Retrieved from http://www. ncbi.nlm.nih.gov/pmc/articles/PMC2566446/pdf/11436481.pdf

46   Guardian Staff. "Euthanasia and assisted suicide laws around the world". *Guardian* (2014, July 17). Accessed June 9th from http://www. theguardian.com/society/2014/jul/17/euthanasia-assisted-suicide-laws-world

reasonable solution for the situation he was in.

e) the physician must have consulted at least one other, independent physician who has seen the patient and has given his written opinion on the requirements of due care, referred to in conditions a) to d), and must have

f) terminated a life or assisted in a suicide with due care. [47]

Children may request euthanasia

In the current Termination of Life on Request and Assisted Suicide Act (2002), children as young as 12 are permitted to receive euthanasia or assisted suicide.[48] However, the legislation that passed follows the Netherlands' Medical Treatment Contracts Act, and parental consent is required for persons under the age of sixteen. In effect, sixteen-year-olds can choose to be euthanized, but parents have to be involved in the discussion.[49] If a patient falls into semi-consciousness just before a scheduled euthanasia procedure, and if there are still signs of suffering, the doctor may perform euthanasia despite the patient's lowered consciousness. A review committee would then assess whether the physician

---

47 'Explanation of the Dutch Law'. *World Federation of Right to Die Societies*. Retrieved on July 5th from http://www.worldrtd.net/ explanation-dutch-law

48 Termination of Life on Request and Assisted Suicide (Review Procedures) Act 2002. Retrieved from http://www.eutanasia.ws/ documentos/Leyes/Internacional/Holanda%20Ley%202002.pdf

49 'Netherlands, first country to legalize euthanasia'. *Bulletin of the World Health Organization* (2001), p.79. Retrieved from http://www. ncbi.nlm.nih.gov/pmc/articles/PMC2566446/pdf/11436481.pdf

who performed the euthanasia fulfilled the statutory due care criteria.[50] The law also contains a section for advance directives. An individual can request euthanasia at some future date when they may find themselves in state that they would now regard as unbearable and offering no prospect of improvement. This document is a request to the patient's physician which contains clear and unambiguous expressions of their wishes.[51] It should be noted that this represents state-endorsed killing of a person who may not presently wish to die, in effect the loss of the right to change your mind when finally experiencing a reality which you had fearfully anticipated at some time in the past.

Belgium

Euthanasia was legalized in Belgium in 2002. The law permits euthanasia when a patient is undergoing intractable and unbearable pain or suffering, whether physical or psychological. It is important to note that Belgium's law does not refer to individuals requesting euthanasia on account of a "terminal illness", only suffering. Patients can also be euthanized if they have clearly given their consent before entering a coma or a similar vegetative state.[52] Regarding assisted suicide, the law states that a physician must be present during the patient's last moments; however the method of suicide is not specified. By contrast, the law in Oregon

---

50   Euthanasia, assisted suicide and non-resuscitation on request. *The Government of Netherlands.* Retrieved from http://www.government.nl/issues/euthanasia/euthanasia-assisted-suicide-and-non-resuscitation-on-request

51   "Netherlands, first country to legalize euthanasia", p. 79.

52   Euthanasia and assisted suicide laws around the world. *Guardian* (2014, July 17) Accessed June 9th from http://www.theguardian.com/society/2014/jul/17/euthanasia-assisted-suicide-laws-world

stipulates that the physician is only responsible for prescribing drugs, and does not need to be present at the patient's death.[53] In February 2014 the Belgian Parliament voted to include terminally-ill children within the terms of this law. The law effectively does away with age restrictions on euthanasia, despite the requirement for the consent of the child's parents and a medical professional. Children with a terminal and incurable illness, and who are near death, and suffering from "constant and unbearable physical" pain, may now participate in Belgium's euthanasia regime.[54]

Luxembourg

In February 2008 Luxembourg became the third country to legalize euthanasia. Prime Minister Jean-Claude Juncker's Social Christian Party was strongly against the bill.[55] While voting was taking place on the bill, the country's head of state, Grand Duke Henri, announced that he would refuse to sign the euthanasia bill into law. To circumvent his opposition Parliament amended the Constitution to eliminate the Grand Duke's power to veto legislation.[56] Most of the legislation is modelled on the Dutch law, except for the age at which a person may request euthanasia. In Luxembourg an individual must be at least eighteen to

---

53   Euthanasia and assisted suicide laws. *Guardian*.

54   "Belgium passes law extending euthanasia to children of all ages". *Guardian* (Feb. 13, 2014) Retrieved from http://www.theguardian. com/world/2014/feb/13/belgium-law-extends-euthanasia-children-all-ages

55   Julien Ponthus, "Luxembourg Parliament adopts euthanasia law." Reuters. (Feb.20, 2008). Retrieved from http://www.reuters.com/ article/2008/02/20/us-luxembourg-euthanasia-idUSL2011983320080220

56   J. Nicol, M. Tiedemann, D. Valiquet. "Euthanasia and Assisted Suicide: International Experiences". Library of Parliament Research Publications (25 Oct. 2013). http://www.parl.gc.ca/content/lop/researchpublications/2011-67-e.htm#ftn83

be euthanized. In the Netherlands the minimum age is twelve, while in Belgium there is no age restriction.

Colombia

On May 20th 1997, the Supreme Court of Colombia ruled that penalties for mercy killings should be removed from the country's criminal legislation and doctors ought to be permitted to end patients' lives by euthanasia.[57] Since this decision, Colombia has been in a legal grey area when it comes to acceptable practices for physicians. The court stated that "without clear rules and precise procedures, doctors do not know exactly when they are committing a crime and when they are contributing to the realization of a fundamental right."[58] Many opposed this decision because of its dangers and corruption in the courts. Nearly twenty years later, in April 2015, Health Ministry authorities began to present guidelines for Colombian doctors on the practice of euthanasia. The past two decades have been very challenging for physicians as they have routinely refused to practise euthanasia, partly for ethical reasons, but also for fear of facing criminal charges.[59]

Where Is Physician-Assisted Suicide Legal?

Assisted suicide is legal in the Netherlands, Albania, Switzerland, Belgium, and Luxembourg. While not

---

57   Republic of Colombia Constitutional Court, Sentence # c-239/97, Ref. Expedient # D-1490 (May 20, 1997).

58   Sabrina Martina. "Colombia to Finalize Euthanasia Law in March". *Pan Am Post* (February 19, 2015) Retrieved from http:// panampost.com/sabrina-martin/2015/02/19/colombia-to-finalize-euthanasia-law-in-march/

59   Sabrina Martina. "Colombia to Finalize Euthanasia Law in March."

strictly speaking legal, assisted suicide may also be practised in certain circumstances in Switzerland, provided the motive is unselfish.[60] In the United States, physician-assisted suicide is legal in Oregon, Washington and Vermont, and has been ambiguously decriminalized in Montana. Assisted suicide differs from euthanasia in that it involves providing the means and instructions for a person to commit suicide, but does not involve the physician administering a lethal injection to bring about the person's death.

Oregon

Oregon passed the Death with Dignity Act on October 27, 1997, allowing terminally-ill state residents to end their lives through the voluntary self-administration of lethal medications, expressly prescribed by a physician for that purpose. The referendum in November 1994 on whether to implement the Act passed by a margin of 51 to 49 per cent. A subsequent ban delayed the implementation of the Act until October 27, 1997. In the election of November 1997, a proposition was placed on the ballot to repeal the Act. This time voters chose to retain the Act by a margin of 60 to 40 per cent.[61] The public was still divided on this law, despite having voted for its adoption.

---

60 Guardian Staff. "Euthanasia and assisted suicide laws around the world". *Guardian* (July 17, 2014). Accessed June 9th, 2015 from http://www.theguardian.com/society/2014/jul/17/euthanasia-assisted-suicide-laws-world. See also Alexander Walzl, et al. *Platon Youth Forum 2009: Euthanasia* (2009) http://www.echa-oesterreich.at/Archiv/platon09/downloads/workshops/ws3/portfolio_ws3.pdf

61 "About the Death With Dignity Act". Oregon Health Authority. Retrieved from https://public.health.oregon.gov/ProviderPartnerResources/EvaluationResearch/DeathwithDignityAct/Pages/faqs.aspx

According to the Act, individuals qualify for physician-assisted suicide when they are 1) eighteen years of age or older; 2) residents of Oregon; 3) capable of making and communicating health care decisions for themselves and; 4) diagnosed with a terminal illness that will lead to death within six months. This final criterion is determined on the basis of a physician's opinion.[62]

Washington

In Washington, the Death with Dignity Act came into force on March 5th, 2009. This act allows terminally-ill adults seeking to end their life to request lethal doses of medication from medical and osteopathic physicians. These terminally-ill patients must be Washington residents who have fewer than six months to live.[63] According to the Act,

> an adult who is 18 years or older, who is competent, is a resident of Washington state, and has been determined by the attending physician and consulting physician to be suffering from a terminal disease, and who has voluntarily expressed his or her wish to die, may make a written request for medication that the patient may self-administer to end his or her life in a humane and dignified manner ....[64]

---

62 "About the Death With Dignity Act".

63 Death with Dignity Act. Washington State Department of Health. Retrieved from http://www.doh.wa.gov/YouandYourFamily/ IllnessandDisease/DeathwithDignityAct

64 The Washington Death With Dignity Act. *Washington State Legislature.* Chapter 70.245 RCW. Retrieved from http://app.leg.wa.gov/ rcw/default.aspx?cite=70.245&full=true

Montana

On December 31, 2009, the Montana Supreme Court changed the legal status of assisted suicide in that state. Its ruling stipulated that rights granted under the state's living will law, The Rights of the Terminally Ill Act, effectively permit physician "aid in dying." However, the court did not explicitly legalize assisted suicide, but merely declared that doctors can cite the patient's request as a defence if charged with assisting a suicide or murder.[65] In effect the Court sidestepped the larger question of whether assisted suicide is a right guaranteed under the state's Constitution.[66] This is not a reassuring legal climate for a euthanasia-minded physician.

Vermont

The Patient Choice and Control at End of Life Act (Act 39) was enacted in May 2013. The statute provides Vermont residents facing a terminal disease with the option of receiving from their physician medication to hasten their death. Patients qualify for assisted suicide if they are "suffering from an incurable and irreversible disease that would, within reasonable medical judgment, result in death within six months. The patient must be capable of making a voluntary, informed health-care decision, and can self-administer the prescribed dose".[67]

---

65   Montana Death With Dignity Act. Patients Rights Council. Retrieved from http://www.patientsrightscouncil.org/site/montana/ - Official Bill for Montana Death With Dignity Act 2008 - http://leg.mt.gov/bills/2015/BillPdf/SB0202.pdf (Review)

66   "Montana Ruling Bolsters Doctor-Assisted Suicide". *New York Times*. (Dec.31, 2009) Retrieved from http://www.nytimes.com/2010/01/01/us/01suicide.html

67   Patient Choice and Control at End of Life Act (Act 39). Vermont Department of Health Agency of Human Services. Retrieved from http://healthvermont.gov/family/end_of_life_care/patient_choice.aspx#law

Switzerland

Under Swiss law euthanasia is illegal; however, assisted suicide is allowed in some cases. Article 115 of the Swiss Criminal Code defines assisted suicide as a crime only if the motive is "selfish". It therefore condones assisted suicide for altruistic reasons.[68] In most cases the permissibility of altruistic assisted suicide cannot be overridden by a duty to save life. Article 115 does not require that a physician be involved, nor that the patient be terminally ill. It only requires that the motive be unselfish.[69] This is a curious law which has created much dispute and conflict.

Switzerland has also allowed the establishment of organizations such as Dignitas and Exit, which provide assisted dying services at a high cost.[70] In October 2009 the Swiss cabinet submitted two legislative proposals for consideration, one for tighter regulation of assisted suicide and the other for an outright ban. The Federal Council decided against introducing specific criminal provisions targeting assisted suicide, but stressed its commitment to discouraging suicide and improving palliative care.[71]

---

68   311.0 Swiss Criminal Code of 21 December 1937, https://www.admin.ch/opc/en/classified-compilation/19370083/index.html#a115
S.A.Hurst and A. Mauron (2003). "Assisted suicide and euthanasia in Switzerland: allowing a role for non-physicians." *BMJ*, 326(7383), 271–3.

69   Hurst and Mauron, "Assisted suicide and euthanasia in Switzerland", 271-3.

70   "Euthanasia and assisted suicide laws around the world". Guardian (2014, July 17). Accessed June 9th from http://www.theguardian.com/society/2014/jul/17/euthanasia-assisted-suicide-laws-world

71   'Assisted suicide: strengthening the right of self-determination: The Federal Council continues to support suicide prevention and palliative care'. Swiss Federal Department of Justice and Police (2011). Retrieved from http://www.ejpd.admin.ch/ejpd/en/home/aktuell/news/2011/2011-06-29.html

To sum up, **euthanasia,** as opposed to **assisted suicide,** is still illegal in Switzerland, as well as in every state of the U.S. including Oregon, Montana, Washington and Vermont.

Conclusion

After reviewing the legislation in various jurisdictions across the world, we note that the great majority of countries continue to prohibit both euthanasia and assisted suicide. As Canada debates this issue, we need to learn from the experience of other jurisdictions about the complications that will inevitably arise. We need also to learn from the responses in other jurisdictions to these complications. Most important is the experience of those jurisdictions where assisted suicide is already legal, in order to take effective measures to protect vulnerable people from having their lives ended without their knowledge or consent, as regularly happens in the Netherlands and Belgium. The experience of assisted suicide, and euthanasia, in these other jurisdictions is more fully explored in Chapter Four.

Chapter 4 *

The experience of jurisdictions which have legalized assisted suicide or euthanasia

Assisted suicide and euthanasia have been legalized, formally or informally, by ten jurisdictions[1] in the past 25 years. We now have extensive data on the impact of legalization in four of those jurisdictions.[2] From this data we can now answer the questions, how has legalization affected people who are older, people with disabilities, and those with mental illness or depression? Does the creation of a legal right to die prevent some individuals from exercising their right to live? There is evidence from the Netherlands that a significant number of those who die by euthanasia do so without making an explicit request. These deaths are continually ignored, excused or justified by supporters of euthanasia and physician-assisted suicide. In the words of the Remmelink Report: "The committee first of all observes that in those cases where no request is made for termination of life, the active intervention of the physician is often unavoidable due to the patient's state of agony."[3] Dutch ethicist,

---

** Chapter 4 written with the assistance of Christina Holmquist.*

1   The Netherlands, Belgium, Luxembourg, Albania, Colombia, Switzerland, Oregon, Washington, Montana and Vermont. In 2016 Canada will become the 11th.

2   The Netherlands, Belgium, Oregon and Washington.

3   Quoted in G. Van Loenen . *Do You Call This a Life? Blurred Boundaries in the Netherlands' Right-to-Die Laws*. London: Ross Lattner Educational Consultants: London, 2015, p. 14.

Theo Boer, who was formerly involved in drafting the euthanasia legislation, now believes "we were wrong -- terribly wrong, in fact."[4] He advises: "at the very least, wait for an honest and intellectually satisfying analysis of the reasons behind the explosive increase in the numbers. Is it because the law should have had better safeguards? Or is it because the mere existence of such a law is an invitation to see assisted suicide and euthanasia as a normality instead of a last resort? Before those questions are answered, don't go there."[5]

The steady rise in euthanasia deaths after legalization

The rise in the number of deaths by euthanasia in the Netherlands referred to by Dr. Boer in his interview is also evident in other jurisdictions where euthanasia or assisted suicide is permitted. This rise, as well as the lack of adherence to the legal safeguards among physicians, the changed perception of people with disabilities, the danger to those who suffer from psychiatric illnesses or depression, and the ethical dilemmas that euthanasia forces upon nurses, physicians, and hospitals, which we document below, are causes for legitimate concern about the legalization of assisted suicide and euthanasia.

Personal autonomy vs "intolerable suffering" vs the physician's choice

The chief argument for legalizing euthanasia in North America is the paramount value of personal autonomy –

---

4 Quoted in Steve Doughty, "Don't make. our mistake: As assisted suicide goes to Lords, Dutch watchdog who once backed euthanasia warns UK of 'slippery slope' to mass deaths", *Daily Mail*, 9 July 2014.

5 Theo Boer, quoted in Steve Doughty. "Don't make our mistake".

the right to choose, without interference, when and where I shall die. In Europe the chief argument is the relief of intolerable suffering. While there is considerable force in both these arguments, it has often been demonstrated that when the patient is given proper care, the demand for assisted suicide evaporates. There is a third category of those who receive assistance in dying: those who do not make any explicit request for it. This category is not often discussed, either in the media or by physicians, perhaps because it qualifies as murder or manslaughter rather than euthanasia. In the Netherlands, it has rarely resulted in the successful prosecution of the physician responsible. The mild sentences occasionally handed down have been accompanied by virtual apologies from the Dutch judges.[6]

The Netherlands

The Remmelink Report

Holland has a lengthy history of euthanasia, tolerating it and collecting data on it, decades before legislation was passed permitting it under the law. As early as 1991, the Remmelink Committee, established by the Dutch government the previous year, released a report on the number and nature of deaths from euthanasia and assisted suicide.[7] This document reported

---

6   John Griffiths, Alex Bood, Heleen Weyers. *Euthanasia and Law in the Netherlands.* Amsterdam: Amsterdam University Press, 1998, p. 273, pp. 2445, 273.

7   P.J. van der Maas, J.M.M. van Delden and L. Pijnenborg,*Medische Beslissingen Rond Het Levenseinde. I: Rapport van de Commissie Onderzoek Medische Praktijk inzake Euthanasie. II: Het Onderzoek voor de Commissie Medische Praktijk inzake Euthanasie (Medical Decisions about the End of Life: I: Report of the Committee to Study the Medical Practice Concerning Euthanasia. II: The Study for the Committee of Medical Practice Concerning Euthanasia).* The Hague: SDU Publishers, Plantijnstraat, 2 vols., 1991. (Hereafter: Remmelink Report), Vol. 1, p. 13.

approximately 2300 deaths per year at the time the report was released, due to active euthanasia, as well as 400 cases of physician-assisted suicide and 1000 cases of active euthanasia without consent.[8] In no less than fourteen per cent of the latter cases the patient was "fully able...to sum up the situation and decide upon it in an adequate way." In a further eleven per cent the patient was partly able to do so, but again no consent was obtained.[9]

Euthanasia performed without explicit request

Besides the significant incidence of euthanasia committed without the patient's request, the committee found that there were at least 25,000 cases annually in which life-prolonging treatment was withdrawn or withheld without consent. While it is true that a large proportion of these patients were unable to conceive or express their will, in 27 per cent of the cases where morphine was administered in such a way that almost certainly there was an intention to shorten life, and that intention was realized, yet "the decision was not discussed with the fully competent patient."[10] Equally disturbing findings of the Remmelink Report were about physicians failing to report, or misreporting, their activities concerning euthanasia. Through interviews it was determined that in close to twenty per cent of

---

8   *Remmelink Report*, vol. I, p. 13. We are grateful to Gerbert van Loenen for help with references to the Remmelink Report and other Dutch-language sources.

9   *Remmelink Report*, vol. I, pp. 13, 15; vol. II, p. 49.

10   *Remmelink Report*, vol. II, pp. 61, 147, Elsewhere in the report, reference is made to the figure 22,500 (vol. I, p. 16) as the number of cases in which life-prolonging treatment is withdrawn or withheld, without noting the discrepancy.

cases general practitioners did not consult a colleague before administering euthanasia. Only 59 per cent of the doctors interviewed thought that the requirement of a written report was important. The great majority (two-thirds to three-quarters) of general practitioners and specialists issued death certificates declaring that the euthanasia deaths were due to natural causes; this they did in the face of legislation defining euthanasia as an unnatural cause of death. Furthermore, where the physician actively terminated life without the patient's explicit request, a certificate of natural death was issued in virtually every instance.[11] This practice has since fortunately declined. Here we are reminded of the irony that the Quebec euthanasia law would force physicians to misrepresent the immediate cause of death on the death certificate by making no reference to the fact of euthanasia.[12]

People euthanized without their request

In 2005, out of a total of 2410 people who died by euthanasia or physician-assisted suicide in the Netherlands, more than 560 were given lethal drugs without their explicit request.[13] Compared to the figure uncovered by the Remmelink Committee fourteen years earlier, this represents a welcome reduction. It nonetheless translates into 0.4 per cent of the total deaths that year from euthanasia, *without request*.[14] A total of 1.7

---

11   *Remmelink Report,* vol. I, pp. 25-6.

12   Sharon Kirkey. "Death be not honest". *National Post,* Sept. 5, 2015, p. A4.

13   A. Van der Heide, B. Onwuteaka-Philipsen, M. Rurup , H. Buiting, J. van Delden, et al. "End of Life Practices in the Netherlands under the Euthanasia Act". *NEJM* 2007; 356: 1957-65.

14   Van der Heide et al. "End of Life Practices in the Netherlands".

per cent of all deaths in the Netherlands were due to euthanasia. Though these figures seem relatively low, 7.1 per cent of all the deaths also involved continuous deep sedation with the possibility of hastening death.[15] The same study also showed that a minimum of twenty per cent of deaths by euthanasia went unreported.[16] It also confirms the apprehension expressed by Dutch researchers that "physicians who are still willing to end life without a patient's explicit request may be engaging in these practices frequently."[17]

Regarding the practice of continuous deep sedation, the 2009 guidelines released by the Royal Dutch Medical Academy state, "in principle there is no artificial administration of fluids in the case of continuous sedation."[18] Between 2005 and 2011 the number of deaths accompanied by palliative sedation averaged 5.7 per cent of all deaths in Dutch general practice.[19] Although palliative sedation is a legitimate treatment for pain and suffering as a patient approaches death, the fact that the Dutch guidelines do not encourage administration of fluids – meaning water -- during sedation suggests that this method may well be

---

15   Van der Heide et al. "End of Life Practices in the Netherlands".

16   Van der Heide et al. "End of Life Practices in the Netherlands".

17   Bregie D. Onwuteaka-Philipsen et al. "Euthanasia and other end-of-life decisions in the Netherlands in 1990, 1995, and 2001". *The Lancet*. 2 Aug. 2003; 362 (9381): pp. 395-9.http://image.thelancet.com/ extras/03art3297web.pdf

18   Royal Dutch Medical Association (KNMG). Guideline for Palliative Sedation. Utecht, The Netherlands: January 2009, p. 6. http:// knmg.artsennet.nl/Publicaties/KNMGpublicatie/66978/Guideline-for-palliative-sedation-2009.htm.

19   G. Donker, F. Slotman P. Spreeuwenberg, and A. Francke. Palliative sedation in Dutch general practice from 2005-2011. *British Journal of General Practice* October 2013, p. 669.

used to hasten patients' deaths besides relieving their symptoms. This is comparable to Quebec's new Act, which expressly sets up "terminal palliative sedation" as a means of "assisted dying".[20]

Euthanasia for children and for those suffering from depression

In 2001 a Dutch law came into force allowing children between the ages of twelve and sixteen to receive euthanasia with the consent of their parents.[21] Children who are sixteen or seventeen can receive euthanasia without their parents' consent, but must involve them in the decision-making process.[22] By 2002, euthanasia was no longer limited to people with a terminal illness or even physical suffering. The legal phrase "suffering hopelessly and unbearably" extends to those with psychological suffering, including depression.[23] It is also acceptable to give an incompetent patient euthanasia if there is an advance directive, written by the patient at an earlier time, for this action.[24] These examples show how euthanasia regulations in the Netherlands have expanded to include more and more categories of people.

---

20   *An Act Respecting End-of-Life Care*, RSQ c S-32.0001, s 1 [*Act*] Chap. I.3 (5), chap.IV (24-5). http://www.assnat.qc.ca/en/travaux-parlementaires/projets-loi/projet-loi-52-40-1.html

21   Government of the Netherlands website. http://www.government.nl/issues/euthanasia/euthanasia-assisted-suicide-and-non-resuscitation-on-request, Accessed on July 31, 2015.

22   http://www.government.nl/issues/euthanasia/euthanasia-assisted-suicide-and-non-resuscitation-on-request

23   http://www.government.nl/issues/euthanasia/euthanasia-assisted-suicide-and-non-resuscitation-on-request

24   http://www.government.nl/issues/euthanasia/euthanasia-assisted-suicide-and-non-resuscitation-on-request

According to a report by the Royal Dutch Medical Association in 2011,

> the Regional Review Committees on Euthanasia have on multiple occasions found that "due care" was taken in cases where the unbearable suffering was caused by an accumulation of various old-age afflictions or a combination of factors, and in which the individual ailments were neither life threatening nor fatal. Physicians have been able to make a sufficiently credible case to these review committees, which are charged with testing physicians' actions against the Euthanasia Law, case law and in light of scientifically supported medical insights and medical ethics standards, that these cases equally involved unbearable and lasting suffering. The KNMG [Royal Dutch Medical Association] therefore concludes that the current statutory framework and the concept of suffering are broader than their interpretation and application by many physicians today.[25]

When euthanasia was first permitted in the Netherlands, it was not intended to include newborn babies.

The Groningen Protocol for terminating the life of newborns

In 2005 a group of doctors at the Groningen University Medical Centre in the Netherlands wrote guidelines

---

25   Koninklijke Nederlandsche Maatschapptij tot bevordering der Geneeskunst (KNMG -- Royal Dutch Medical Association). The role of the physician in the voluntary termination of life. June 2011, p. 23.

for the termination of life in newborns, even though the law against ending the lives of infants was still on the books.[26] In reality active euthanasia for infants was being practised as early as 1995, when a doctor who ended the life of an infant with Spina Bifida, hydrocephalus, lower body paralysis and deformity was taken to court, but acquitted because he "acted in accordance with scientifically sound medical understanding and in accordance with current medical ethical standards."[27] The court's verdict of not guilty for the doctors charged in this case and one other had far-reaching implications. Effectively it made the euthanasia of infants for whom medical treatment was deemed pointless, and whom the doctors declared to be suffering unbearably, exempt from prosecution in the Netherlands.

When doctors began to use the Groningen Protocol to select infants for euthanasia, they also began to euthanize those who would be able to survive on their own but whose poor "quality of life" was expected to cause them severe suffering in the future. Ironically, "the Groningen protocol regulates life termination in babies with a longer life expectancy."[28] B.A. Manninen, a supporter of the Groningen protocol, even expressed concerns that as a consequence of the protocol physicians are now making quality of life judgments on their tiny patients. Manninen had

---

26   B.D. Onwuteaka-Philipsen, J.K.M. Gevers, A. van der Heide et al. *Evaluatie wet toetsing levensbeëindiging op verzoek en hulp bij zelfdoding* [*Evaluation of the Dutch Euthanasia Act of 2002*]. Den Haag: ZonMw, 2007, p. 112.

27   De zaak-Prins, Hof Amsterdam November 7 1995, TvGR 1996, pp. 30-6 [The Prins case].

28   De zaak-Prins, Hof Amsterdam, pp. 30-6.

only supported infant euthanasia when the infant in question was certain to die in the near future and euthanasia merely shortened a very short life. It is her conviction that quality of life judgements should never be made.

> If the Groningen physicians have commenced making quality of life judgments, they have strayed away from the original purpose of the Protocol, and this, I believe, may have concerning ethical implications…. If the infant did have a possible future ahead of her, I would be more hesitant to condone a legal practice that begins to make quality of life judgments, for such judgments can be, and have been, subject to error.[29]

The Groningen Protocol specifies that before an infant life can be ended several conditions must be met. They include "extreme and sustained suffering and poor quality of life in terms of functional disability, pain, discomfort, poor prognosis and hopelessness… predicted lack of self-sufficiency… predicted inability to communicate… expected hospital dependency… expectation of prolonged survival."[30] There are five additional requirements: "…diagnosis and prognosis must be certain…hopeless and unbearable suffering

---

29   Quoted in T.H. Rob de Jong. "Deliberate termination of life of newborns with spina bifida, a critical reappraisal". *Childs Nerv Syst* Jan. 2008;24 (1):13-28. See also B.A. Manninen. "A case for justified non-voluntary active euthanasia: exploring the ethics of the Groningen Protocol."*J Med Ethics* 32 (11); Nov. 2006: 643-51, p. 650.

30   S. Barry. "Quality of Life and Myelomeningocele: An Ethical and Evidence Based Analysis of the Groningen Protocol." *Pediatric Neurosurgery* 2010; 46:409-414, p. 410.

must be present... the first and second requirements must be confirmed by at least one physician not involved in the patient's care... both parents must give informed consent... the procedure ending the patient's life itself must be performed in accordance with the accepted medical standard."[31]

Although these conditions sound very exacting, and would seem to apply only to infants in the worst possible circumstances, they are essentially subjective, and can be applied to infants who are not suffering at present but who the physician assumes will likely suffer in the future. According to Eduard Verhagen the Groningen Protocol is designed to "include patients who are not dependent on intensive medical treatment but for whom a very poor quality of life, associated with sustained suffering, is predicted."[32] Particularly disturbing is the finding that while fifteen to twenty infants are euthanized every year in the Netherlands, on average only three of the cases are reported, despite the legal requirement to do so.[33]

Infants with spina bifida (MMC)

A study of the deaths of 22 infants who received euthanasia, reported that all of them were in pain.[34] However, the amount of pain that infants with spina bifida experience is insufficiently researched; indeed,

---

31   S. Barry. "Quality of Life and Myelomeningocele", p. 410

32   E. Verhagen. "The Groningen Protocol- Euthanasia in Severely Ill Newborns". *NEJM* 2005; 352: 10, p. 960.

33   Verhagen. "Groningen Protocol", p. 962.

34   T.H. Rob de Jong. Deliberate termination of life of newborns with spina bifida, a critical reappraisal. Childs Nerv Syst 2008; 24:13-28, p. 18.

there are no known studies on this topic.[35] In the words of Dr. Zachary, a pediatric surgeon: "I personally have seen little evidence that the babies have pain in the newborn period, nor have I found them unable to sleep."[36] In a study of 44 newborns with MMC (spina bifida), only 25 per cent needed analgesics or anticonvulsants and 50 per cent were given drugs during their dying period.[37] A Dutch study of babies with spina bifida concluded that they were not in pain at all, and that any pain there may have been was easily amenable to medication.[38]

Physicians and family members tend to overestimate the burden that a disability will cause. Studies of how patients with MMC rate their quality of life show that there is a major discrepancy between how others predict they will rate their quality of life and how they themselves rate it. One study found that 24 per cent of MMC patients were dissatisfied with their lives. This is actually a *lower* percentage than that of the control group who were *not* suffering from MMC. Among the control group 28 per cent said they were dissatisfied with their

---

35   T.H. Rob de Jong. Deliberate termination of life of newborns with spina bifida, p. 18.

36   R.B. Zachary. Life with spina bifida. BMJ 1977; 1460–2, p. 1461.

37   E. Delight, J. Goodall. Babies with spina bifida treated without surgery: parents' views on home versus hospital care. BMJ 1988; 297:1230–3, p. 1231.

38   E.J.O. Kompanje, T.H.R. de Jong, W.F.M. Arts, J.J. Roteveel. "Problematische basis voor 'uitzichtloos en ondraaglijk lijden' als criterium voor actieve levensbeëindiging bij pasgeborenen met spina bifida". [Problematical basis for 'hopeless and unbearable suffering' as a criterion for active euthanasia in newborns with spina bifida] Ned Tijdschr Geneeskd 2005 10 September;r49:2067-9.

lives.[39] With up-to-date medical care, such as shunts, which are necessary for 86 per cent of survivors, MMC is a more manageable condition than ever before.[40] A study by Hunt and Oakeshott found that out of 117 individuals born with spina bifida, 54 survived at least to age 35.[41] Out of these 54, 22 were able to live independently, and a further twelve lived in accommodations where help was available when required.[42] Only twenty were severely disabled and needed daily help.[43] The study made no reference to patients experiencing the "unbearable suffering" referred to by the Groningen Protocol.[44] Despite doctors' predictions that an infant born with MMC will likely be unable to talk, the majority of patients with MMC do have that ability.[45]

It is true that children born with spina bifida will receive more than the average medical care. Is this a justification for euthanizing them?[46] Some doctors have predicted that infants with spina bifida could need up to 60 surgeries in the first year of their life, when in reality

---

39   H.A. Barf, M.W.M Post, M. Verhoef, A. Jennekens-Schinkel, R.H. Gooskens, A.J. Prevo."Life satisfaction of young adults with spina bifida". Developmental Medicine and Child Neurology 2007; 49: 458-63, pp. 460, 461.

40   S. Barry. Quality of Life and Myelomeningocele: An Ethical and Evidence Based Analysis of the Groningen Protocol. Pediatric Neurosurgery 2010; 46:409-14, p. 413.

41   G.M. Hunt, P. Oakeshott. "Outcome in people with open spina bifida at age 35: prospective community based cohort study". BMJ 2003; 326:1365–6.

42   Hunt, Oakeshott. "Outcome in people with open spina bifida at age 35".

43   Hunt, Oakeshott. "Outcome in people with open spina bifida at age 35".

44   S. Barry. "Quality of Life and Myelomeningocele: An Ethical and Evidence Based Analysis of the Groningen Protocol". Pediatric Neurosurgery 2010; 46:409-414, p. 413.

45   Barry. "Quality of Life and Myelomeningocele", p. 413.

46   Barry. "Quality of Life and Myelomeningocele", p. 413.

they will likely need only three or four.[47] Physicians cannot always accurately predict a spina bifida patient's future condition and need for care, especially not immediately after birth.[48] Physicians often present worst-case scenarios, and parents are then obliged to make up their minds on the basis of hopeless-sounding prognoses.[49] The Groningen Protocol operates as little more than an escape route for parents wishing to shed the burden of caring for a child with a disability. It also functions as a rationale for doctors, hospitals and governments who want to minimize the care of the disabled.

Belgium

The non-reporting of euthanasia deaths

If we are to believe the official reports of the Federal Control and Evaluation Committee, the practice of euthanasia in Belgium is in conformity with the law, and there have been no cases of abuse. These reports are, however, limited to the data that physicians report on their own performance of euthanasia. Anonymous surveys of physicians for the purpose of determining actual reported and unreported cases of euthanasia in Flanders, Belgium were carried out in 2007, and 2013. The survey from 2007 revealed that, of the deaths that occurred between 1 June 2007 and 30 November

---

47   T.H Rob de Jong. Deliberate termination of life of newborns with spina bifida, a critical reappraisal. Childs Nerv Syst 2008; 24 (1):13-28, p. 19.

48   S. Barry. Quality of Life and Myelomeningocele: An Ethical and Evidence Based Analysis of the Groningen Protocol. Pediatric Neurosurgery 2010; 46:409-414,p. 414.

49   Rob de Jong. Deliberate termination of life of newborns with spina bifida, p. 19.

2007, an estimated 1040 or 1.9 per cent were a result of euthanasia.[50] *Only half of these deaths were reported to the Federal Control and Evaluation Committee.*[51]

The unreported euthanasia deaths tell a different story about the effectiveness of the laws which regulate the practice of euthanasia and the care physicians take to meet these legal requirements. In cases where euthanasia was not reported, the time that euthanasia shortened the individual's life was estimated by the physician to be less than a week (37.3 per cent reported), as opposed to a longer amount of time (74.1 per cent reported), and when the physician did not "perceive the act as euthanasia".[52] Other reasons why physicians did not report euthanasia included administrative burden (17.9 per cent), "legal due care requirements had possibly not all been met" (11.9 per cent). A further nine per cent were of the opinion "that euthanasia is a private matter between physician and patient, [while] 2.3 per cent did not report the case because of possible legal consequences".[53]

The legal criteria for performing euthanasia were more often ignored in the unreported cases. Thus, 87.7 per cent of the unreported cases were performed without a written request in contrast to only 17.6 per

---

50   J. Bilsen, J. Cohen, L. Deliens, F. Mortier, M. Rurup, and T. Smets. Reporting of euthanasia in medical practice in Flanders Belgium: cross sectional analysis of reported and unreported cases. BMedical Journal 2010; 341:c5174, p. 1.
51   Bilsen et al. Reporting of euthanasia in medical practice in Flanders, p. 1.
52   Bilsen et al. Reporting of euthanasia in medical practice in Flanders, pp. 3, 4.
53   Bilsen et al. Reporting of euthanasia in medical practice in Flanders, p. 4.

cent of reported cases. In only 54.6 per cent of the unreported cases were other physicians and palliative caregivers consulted, compared to 97.5 per cent of reported cases. Opioids or sedatives were used in 92.1 per cent of the unreported cases, but only 4.4 per cent of reported cases.[54] In unreported cases, the drugs (opioids and sedatives) were administered 41.3 per cent of the time by nurses alone; while in 97.7 per cent of reported cases the drugs were administered by a physician.[55]

These percentages may not show the full extent of unreported cases. There is a real possibility that among the physicians who did not respond to the survey, a larger proportion performed euthanasia without explicit request than among those who did respond. This is a plausible inference, since people are understandably reluctant to admit their illegal activity. Given that the study was dependent on self-reporting by physicians, it most likely underestimated the extent of unreported euthanasia, and the illegal practices of those who failed to report.

Physician-assisted death without the patient's request

Another survey found that out of 208 physician-assisted deaths, 66 were without an explicit request from the patient.[56] Fully 1.8 per cent of all deaths in Flanders during the study period were a result of

---

54   Bilsen et al. Reporting of euthanasia in medical practice in Flanders, p. 4.

55   Bilsen et al. Reporting of euthanasia in medical practice in Flanders, p. 4.

56   J. Bilsen, K. Chambaere, J. Cohen, L. Deliens, B. Onwuteaka-Philipsen, F. Mortier. Physician assisted deaths under the euthanasia law in Belgium: a population-based survey. CMAJ 2010; 182(9): 895-901, p. 895.

euthanasia without explicit request.[57] The patients who did not make an explicit request most often were over 80 years old (52.7 per cent), were without cancer (67.5 per cent), and died in a hospital (67.1 per cent).[58] The end-of-life decision was discussed with patients who had not explicitly requested euthanasia only 22.1 per cent of the time.[59] The other patients were not even informed of the decision to end their lives.

Why was euthanasia not discussed with the patient?

Among the reasons given for not discussing this decision with the patient were, 1) that the patient was comatose (70.1 per cent); 2) had dementia (21.1 per cent); 3) the decision was in the patient's best interest (17.0 per cent); and 4) the discussion would have been harmful (8.2 per cent).[60] Even if we omit the patients who were comatose or had dementia, we are still left with 8.8 per cent who did not request euthanasia, even though they were competent to request it if that was what they wanted. In 38.2 per cent of the unrequested cases one of the reasons for the decision was "unbearable situation for the family".[61] By contrast, in only 17.0 per cent of cases where there was an explicit request for euthanasia was one of the reasons "unbearable situation for the

57   Bilsen et al. Physician assisted deaths under the euthanasia law in Belgium, p. 895.

58   Bilsen et al. "Physician assisted deaths under the euthanasia law in Belgium", p. 896.

59   Bilsen et al. "Physician assisted deaths under the euthanasia law in Belgium", p. 896.

60   Bilsen et al. "Physician assisted deaths under the euthanasia law in Belgium", p. 896.

61   Bilsen et al. "Physician assisted deaths under the euthanasia law in Belgium", p. 898.

family".[62] The proponents of euthanasia argue that it would only be offered to those who have expressed a personal desire for death. In reality pressure is put on the elderly and those suffering from difficult illnesses by family members and doctors to get them to choose the option that will eliminate them as a burden to their family and society. Other reasons that were prominent in cases lacking explicit request were "wish of the family" (50.1 per cent vs. 25.6 per cent in reported cases), and "life not to be prolonged needlessly" (62.9 per cent vs. 39.9 per cent).[63] Patients who did not explicitly request euthanasia often had a shorter period of treatment for their terminal illness (less than a month in 46.1 per cent of cases) compared to more than six months for the 80.3 per cent of patients who made an explicit request.[64] It should be emphasized that the estimates of life expectancy were made at the discretion of self-reporting doctors. They could be expected to minimize the loss of life which their actions had caused. In reality we have no idea of the living time lost to euthanasia by non-reporting doctors and nurses. The estimated amount of time by which their life was shortened was also less (under 24 hours in 47.9 per cent of cases).[65] These data confirm that euthanasia is not always the choice of the patient and can be a way for family members and hospitals to avoid the responsibility of giving needed care to some of the most vulnerable members of society.

---

62   Bilsen et al. "Physician assisted deaths under the euthanasia law in Belgium", p. 898.
63   Bilsen et al. "Physician assisted deaths under the euthanasia law in Belgium", p. 898.
64   Bilsen et al. "Physician assisted deaths under the euthanasia law in Belgium", p. 897.
65   Bilsen et al. "Physician assisted deaths under the euthanasia law in Belgium", p. 897.

The steady increase in the practice of euthanasia

Euthanasia was legalized in Belgium in 2002.66 A brief overview of the reported euthanasia cases reveals that "the number of reported euthanasia cases increased every year from 0.23 per cent of all deaths in 2002 to 0.49 per cent in 2007."67 As euthanasia became an accepted practice for more illnesses and less of a last resort for unbearable suffering, it markedly increased from 1.9 per cent of all deaths or 69 of the 3623 studied deaths in 2007 to 4.6 per cent or 173 of the 3751 studied deaths in 2013.68 This is a two-and-a-half times increase in six years. The increase comes both from a rise in requests (from 3.5 to 6.0 per cent of all deaths) and from doctors being more willing to grant these requests (56.3 to 76.8 per cent).69 The number of cases where death was hastened without an explicit request by the patient remained disturbingly high at 64, or 1.7 per cent of the 3751 deaths. As late as 2009 the Federal Control and Evaluation Committee still did not suspect that the requirements for due care were being flouted. Not one case involving violation of the requirements has yet

---

66   K. Chambaere, J. Bilsen, J. Cohen, B.D. Onwuteaka-Philipsen, F. Mortier, L. Deliens. "Trends in medical end-of-life decision making in Flanders, Belgium 1998-2001-2007". Med Decis Making 2011; 31 (3):500-10, p. 500.

67   T. Smets, J. Bilsen, J. Cohen, L. Mette, L. Rurup, Deliens . "Legal Euthanasia in Belgium: Characteristics of All Reported Euthanasia Cases". Medical Care 2009; 47(12), p. 1. http://www. worldrtd.net/sites/default/files/u22/Smets_reported%20euthanasia%20 cases_Med%20Care.pdf. Accessed July 23, 2015.

68   K. Chambaere, J. Cohen, F. Mortier, R. Vander Stichele. Recent Trends in Euthanasia and Other End of Life Practices in Belgium. NEJM 2015; 372 (12), p. 1179. http://www.nejm.org/doi/pdf/10.1056/NEJMc1414527.

69   Chambaere et al. "Recent Trends in Euthanasia and Other End of Life Practices in Belgium", p. 1179.

been sent to trial.[70] These findings point to an increased acceptance of euthanasia as an end-of-life option for more types of illnesses among physicians and patients in Flanders.

Originally euthanasia was not intended as a replacement for palliative care. It was justified as an option when palliative care could not adequately manage pain and suffering. Now, however, in Belgium the requirement for palliative care consultations has evidently been waived, with the consequence that palliative care physicians and their teams were not involved in 65 per cent of cases where euthanasia was administered.[71] Between 2001 and 2007 palliative caregivers were only involved in an average of thirteen per cent of cases of euthanasia in Belgium.[72] This percentage has declined every year, with palliative care involvement at 19.3 per cent in 2002/3 and 8.7 per cent in 2007.[73]

The depressed woman who broke her son's heart

Recently the *New Yorker* featured an article on euthanasia in Belgium, focusing on one woman, Godelieva De Troyer who died by euthanasia at the age of 64 after struggling with depression for much of her life and having recently been left by her long-term boyfriend.[74] Her suicide

---

70   T. Smets, J. Bilsen, J. Cohen, M. Rurup, E. Keyser, L. Deliens. "The Medical Practice of Euthanasia in Belgium and the Netherlands: Legal notification, control, and evaluation process". Elsvier Health Policy 2009; 90: 181-7, p. 185.

71   T. Smets, J. Bilsen, J. Cohen, L. Mette, M. Rurup, L. Deliens. "Legal Euthanasia in Belgium: Characteristics of All Reported Euthanasia Cases". *Medical Care* Dec. 2009; 47:12, p. 3.

72   Smets et al. "Legal Euthanasia in Belgium", p. 5.

73   Smets et al. "Legal Euthanasia in Belgium", p. 5.

74   R. Aviv. "The Death Treatment". New Yorker. June 22, 2015, p. 56.

shocked her son Tom, who did not find out about it until afterwards, and was upset that the doctors would even consider her request, given her psychological status and previous ups-and-downs. In fact, Godelieva had difficulty securing the necessary recommendation from three doctors to receive euthanasia. One psychiatrist refused because there were still options available to help with Godelieva's depression and "when Godelieva discussed her grandchildren she became emotional and expressed doubts about her decision to die."[75] Another said that Godelieva's decision was "not mature" and that she went through "ups and downs."[76] Further evidence that Godelieva had not been completely satisfied with her decision was the discarded letter Tom found, which read: "I have not been able to handle the rift with you, Tom. I have loved you very much but you have not seen it as such…I will not see my grandchildren grow up and that causes me pain."[77]

Godelieva is just one example of the many recipients of euthanasia in Belgium who were neither terminally ill nor dying. Apart from depression, people have been euthanized for "autism, anorexia, borderline personality disorder, chronic-fatigue syndrome, partial paralysis, blindness coupled with deafness, and manic depression."[78] In 2013, a 44-year-old, transgendered man was euthanized after failed sex-change surgeries made him feel like "a monster when he looked in the mirror."[79]

---

75   R. Aviv. "The Death Treatment". p. 63.
76   R. Aviv. "The Death Treatment". p. 63.
77   R. Aviv. "The Death Treatment". p. 58.
78   R. Aviv. "The Death Treatment". p. 59.
79   R. Aviv. "The Death Treatment". p. 59.

Dr. Patrick Wyffels, who performs euthanasia eight to ten times a year, acknowledges that "in the days before and after the procedure, he finds it difficult to sleep. 'You spend seven years studying to be a doctor, and all they do is teach you how to get people well -- and then you do the opposite...I am afraid of the power that I have in that moment.'"[80] Herman De Dijin, a philospher who responded to Tom after his mother's death said: "Once the law is there, you have people asking themselves new questions...'Do I really have quality of life? Am I not a burden on others?' He worried that the concept (of human dignity) had been 'reduced to the ability to have certain experiences.'"[81]

The increasing (illegal) involvement of nurses

The abuse of the law in Belgium also extends to how the lethal drugs are administered and who administers them. By law only doctors are permitted to administer euthanasia, yet a survey of nurses on the last patient in their care for whom a life-shortening end-of-life decision was made revealed that nurses' involvement in euthanasia extended much farther than the law allowed.[82] More than a tenth of the nurses who responded (128) reported that a patient received euthanasia (at their request), while nearly a tenth (120) reported that they gave patients lethal drugs *without* their explicit request.[83] In twelve per cent of cases of euthanasia with request the nurse administered the

---

80   R. Aviv. "The Death Treatment". p. 59.
81   R. Aviv. "The Death Treatment". p. 62.
82   J. Bilsen, L. Deliens, E. Inghelbrecht, F. Mortier. "The role of nurses in physician-assisted deaths in Belgium". CMAJ June 15, 2010; 182 (9), p. 905.
83   Bilsen et al. "The role of nurses", p. 905.

lethal drugs.[84] More disturbingly, in 45 per cent of the cases where the patient's life was ended without explicit request, it was a nurse who administered the lethal drugs.[85] The physician did not co-administer in 37 per cent of all cases.[86] The physician was not even present in 58 per cent of the cases in which the nurse administered the lethal drugs.[87] Factors that increased the chances of the nurse administering the lethal drugs include "the absence of an explicit request from the patient, the patient being more than 80-years-old, and the nurse having had a recent experience with life-shortening end-of-life decisions."[88] Although doctors are legally required to discuss the request for euthanasia with the nurse involved, only 64 per cent of nurses were consulted in the decision for euthanasia while only 69 per cent were consulted in the decision to give lethal drugs to a patient without explicit request.[89] Not only is the law being widely flouted, but nurses are being saddled with responsibilities that were never intended for them. As a consequence, some of them are taking the law into their own hands, and going far beyond what the law authorizes.

Euthanizing children

Euthanasia in Belgium was being practised on children in 2008, even though it was not permitted by law until

---

84   Bilsen et al. The role of nurses , p. 905.

85   Bilsen et al. "The role of nurses", p. 905.

86   Bilsen et al. "The role of nurses", p. 907.

87   Bilsen et al. "The role of nurses", p. 907.

88   Bilsen et al. "The role of nurses", p. 907.

89   Bilsen et al. "The role of nurses", p. 907.

February 13, 2014.[90] Out of 165 deaths between June 2007 and November 2008 in Flanders of patients aged between one and seventeen, "drugs were administered to alleviate pain and symptoms with a possible life-shortening effect in 18.2 per cent of all deaths, non-treatment decisions were made in 10.3 per cent and lethal drugs without the patient's explicit request were used in 7.9 per cent."[91] The two most common reasons why end-of-life decisions were made were that "no improvement to be expected" (84.6 per cent) and because there was "low expected quality of life" (61.5 per cent).[92] The parents requested the decision in 30.4 per cent of non-treatment decisions, in 33.3 per cent of the cases of administration of drugs to alleviate pain and symptoms with a possible life-shortening effect, and in 75 per cent of cases of physician-assisted death.[93] At 7.9 per cent, the rate at which lethal drugs were used to bring about these children's deaths was more than double the rate for adults (3.8 per cent).[94] It is clear that adolescent children, with their known vulnerability to depression and suicidal thoughts, are in great danger under the most recent change to the law in Belgium.

---

90 "Belgium Parliament Votes Through Child Euthanasia." BBC News. February 13, 2014. http://www.bbc.com/news/world-europe-26181615. Accessed on August 4, 2015.

91 J. Bilsen, K. Chambaere, J. Cohen, L. Deliens, F. Mortier, G. Pousset. Medical End-of-Life Decisions in Children in Flanders, Belgium A Population-Based Postmortem Survey. Arch Pediatr Adolesc Med. 2010; 164(6):547-553, p. 547.

92 Bilsen et al. Medical End-of-Life Decisions in Children in Flanders, p. 550

93 Bilsen et al. Medical End-of-Life Decisions in Children in Flanders, p. 550.

94 Bilsen et al. Medical End-of-Life Decisions in Children in Flanders, p. 551.

Patients with psychiatric disorders

A new study of patients with psychiatric conditions who requested euthanasia reveals the extent to which psychological suffering is accepted as a qualification for euthanasia.[95] Out of the 100 consecutive requests, 48 were accepted and 35 were carried out.[96] Eleven of the patients whose request was accepted, cancelled or postponed receiving euthanasia.[97] Of the 52 patients whose requests were denied, 38 withdrew their requests before a decision was reached.[98] The most common illness that patients suffered from was major depressive disorder (48 per cent).[99] Individuals with both major depressive disorder and bipolar disorder or a personality disorder accounted for 29 per cent of the requests.[100] Other disorders included post-traumatic stress disorder (thirteen per cent), schizophrenia and other psychotic disorders (fourteen per cent), anxiety disorders (eleven per cent), eating disorders (ten per cent), substance use disorders (ten per cent), somatoform disorders (nine per cent), pervasive developmental disorders (eight per cent,

---

95   L. Thienpont, M. Verhofstadt, T. Van Loon, W. Distelmans, K. Audenaert, P. De Deyn. "Euthanasia requests, procedures and outcomes for 100 Belgian patients suffering from psychiatric disorders: a retrospective, descriptive study. BMJ 2015; 5:e007454, p. 1.

96   Thienpont et al. "Euthanasia requests, procedures and outcomes for 100 Belgium patients", p. 1.

97   Thienpont et al. "Euthanasia requests, procedures and outcomes for 100 Belgium patients", p. 5.

98   Thienpont et al. "Euthanasia requests, procedures and outcomes for 100 Belgium patients", p. 5.

99   Thienpont et al. "Euthanasia requests, procedures and outcomes for 100 Belgium patients", p. 5.

100   Thienpont et al. "Euthanasia requests, procedures and outcomes for 100 Belgium patients", p. 5.

which included seven with autism spectrum disorder and one with ADHD (attention deficit hyperactivity disorder), obsessive compulsive disorders (seven per cent), dissociative disorders (seven per cent), and complicated grief (six per cent).[101]

The many abuses of the law in Belgium

To sum up, the euthanasia law in Belgium is extremely permissive. Even so, there have been many abuses of the law. Almost half the euthanasia cases go unreported. Many of the unreported cases are performed without a written request. Others are done to relieve a burden on the family. Euthanasia may only be performed by a physician, yet nurses are increasingly asked to give the lethal injection. In some cases they are doing it on their own initiative. Yet not one case involving a violation of the law has been sent to trial, which would seem to indicate that the authorities are turning a blind eye to such cases. Euthanasia is increasingly being offered to people whose only medical condition is depression. Depression is a treatable condition, and it is questionable whether anyone in that condition is capable of making a rational request to have their life ended. Adolescent children, with their known vulnerability to depression and suicidal thoughts, are now eligible for euthanasia. Belgium is well on its way down the slippery slope.

Switzerland

Assisted suicide has only become legal in Switzerland thanks to a loophole in the law that permits people

---

101   Thienpont et al. "Euthanasia requests, procedures and outcomes for 100 Belgium patients", p. 5.

to assist others in committing suicide without being charged with a crime. Consequently, those who desire help in committing suicide can obtain that help without the recommendation or involvement of a physician. This unusual situation has opened the way for organizations that promote dying by assisted suicide to flourish in Switzerland. Many "suicide tourists" now come in search of services that are against the law in their own countries. In 2013 a draft bill to regulate and supervise the activities of right-to-die associations in the Canton of Zurich was defeated in the cantonal parliament.[102] Between 2008 and 2012 there were 611 assisted suicide deaths in Switzerland of people classified as "suicide tourists".[103]

Luxembourg

The legislation allowing euthanasia in Luxembourg came into effect on April 1, 2009.[104] The introduction of this law led to a change in the national constitution. When Grand Duke Henri refused to sign the bill, the Luxembourg parliament voted to reduce the Duke's power so that his signature was not required to pass a bill.[105] The law is modelled on Belgium's euthanasia law, and allows physician-assisted suicide as well as euthanasia.[106]

USA

At the time of writing, assisted suicide is legal in Oregon, Washington, Montana, and Vermont. Bills to legalize it

---

102   S. Guthier, J. Mausbach, T. Reisch, C. Bartsch. Suicide tourism: a pilot study on the Swiss phenomenon. Journal of Medical Ethics August 20, 2014, p. 611.

103   Guthier. Suicide tourism, p. 611.

104   R. Watson. Luxembourg is to allow euthanasia from April 1. BMJ 2009; 338: b1248, p. 1.

105   Watson. Luxembourg is to allow euthanasia, p. 2.

106   Watson. Luxembourg is to allow euthanasia, p. 2.

have been introduced in many states. Referendums to legalize assisted suicide have been turned back in several states: California, Massachusetts, Michigan and Maine. Oregon was the first state to permit assisted suicide, in 1997, and thus has accumulated the most data about the practice.[107] Washington's "Death with Dignity Act" is comparatively recent, with the act passing on November 4, 2008 and coming into effect March 5 2009.[108] Physician-assisted suicide became legal in Montana on December 31, 2009 by a ruling from that state's lower court.[109] The ruling freed doctors from criminal prosecution for ending the life of their patient on the basis of a written request.[110] In Vermont, the Patient Choice and Control at the End of Life Act was signed into law on May 20, 2013.[111]

The regulations and reporting procedures are so relaxed in the U.S. that it is hard to be sure how many deaths occur as a result of assisted suicide per year and how well these deaths reflect patients' wishes. There is a lack of follow-up to reports of physician- assisted suicide in Oregon. This is exemplified by a press release from the Oregon Department of Human Services, which says: "The Oregon Department of Human Services has no authority to investigate individual Death with Dignity

---

107   Oregon Public Health Division. Oregon's Death with Dignity Act 2014, p. 1. http://public.health.oregon.gov/ProviderPartnerREsources/EvaluationResearch/DeathwithDignityAct/Documents/year17.pdf

108   Washington State Department of Health Website. http://www.doh.wa.gov/YouandYourFamily/IllnessandDisease/DeathwithDignityAct, Accessed July 30, 2015.

109   Robert Baxter vs. Supreme Court of Montana. Montana Supreme Court, decided 2009. http://www.patientsrightscouncil.org/site/wp-content/uploads/2011/03/Montana_Opinion_12_31_09.pdf

110   Robert Baxter vs. Supreme Court of Montana.

111   Vermont Department of Health Agency of Human Services Website. http://www.healthvermont.gov/family/end_of_life_care/patient_choice.aspx#law, Accessed July 31, 2015.

cases, officials said Friday. The state law authorizing physician-assisted suicide neither requires nor authorizes investigations by DHS, said Barry S. Kast, DHS assistant director for health services"[112].

Oregon

The burden on physicians

A cause for concern, not only in Oregon, but in all areas where assisted suicide and euthanasia are practised, is the emotional stress that direct involvement in this procedure puts on physicians. A study of physicians in Oregon revealed that 24 per cent felt regret for performing euthanasia or physician-assisted suicide.[113] While this is only a minority of the physicians who practised euthanasia or assisted suicide, it is a large enough one to cause serious concern, especially given that the great majority of physicians wish to have nothing to do with euthanasia or assisted suicide. The Oregon Health Division report found that "for some physicians, the process of participating in physician-assisted suicide had a great emotional impact."[114]

Safeguards widely ignored

The four primary proposed safeguards are: 1) the patient must be terminally ill; 2) the patient must initiate and repeat the request for euthanasia; 3) the patient must experience physical suffering or pain; and 4)

112   Oregon Department of Human Services Press Release. No Authority to Investigate Death with Dignity Cases. 4 March 2005, http://www.oregon. gov/dhs/pages/news/2005news/2005-0304a.aspx, accessed July 22, 2015.

113   Oregon Department of Human Services Press Release. No Authority to Investigate.

114   "Oregon's Death with Dignity Act: The First Year's Experience," Oregon Health Division Report, Feb 18, 1999, page 7.

the patient must be evaluated by another physician.[115] However, according to a major study all the safeguards were only followed in one-third of cases.[116]

The story of a woman named Jeanette Hall, who lived in Oregon and met the criteria for assisted suicide, illustrates how the safeguard of being within six months of death does not prevent all those who could live longer from accessing assisted suicide. When Jeanette was diagnosed with cancer in 2000, she was given between six months and one year to live.[117] Her doctor was unwilling to prescribe assisted suicide and encouraged her to undergo chemotherapy and radiation, which she agreed to.[118] In Jeanette's own words: "I am happy to be alive. It is now eleven years later. If my doctor had believed in assisted suicide, I would be dead. I thank him and all my doctors for helping me choose 'life with dignity'."[119]

Ill people are being pressured to accept euthanasia

There is disturbing evidence that seriously ill people are being pressured into accepting euthanasia in order to save health dollars. When Barbara Wagner's lung cancer returned after previously going into remission, her insurance company refused her request to cover the

115   E.J. Emanuel. "The Practice of Euthanasia and Physician-assisted Suicide in the United States: Adherence to Proposed Safeguards and Effects on Physicians". JAMA 1998; 280 (6), 507-13.

116   (34%). Emanuel. "The Practice of Euthanasia and Physician-assisted Suicide".

117   J. Hall. "She pushed for a legal right to die, and- thankfully- was rebuffed". Boston Globe October 4, 2011. http://www.boston.com/bostonglobe/editorial_opinion/letters/articles/2011/10/04/she_pushed_for_legal_right_to_die_and___thankfully___was_rebuffed/. Accessed July 29, 2015.

118   J. Hall. "She pushed for a legal right to die".

119   J. Hall. "She pushed for a legal right to die".

cost of expensive medication that could have extended her life. This refusal stemmed from the Oregon Health Plan's policy of only funding the treatment of patients with a better-than five per cent chance of survival for longer than five years.[120] Instead of agreeing to pay for the life-extending treatment, the insurance company suggested assisted suicide pills (cost: $50) as part of their "palliative" or comfort care plan.[121]

Randy Stroup was also denied potentially life-saving chemotherapy for his prostate cancer by the Oregon Health Plan which is administered in Lane County by the Lane Individual Practice Association.[122] He received a letter from them saying they would not cover the cost of the chemotherapy but they would pay for physician-assisted suicide at a much lower cost. Randy fought back, and in the end obtained the chemotherapy treatment that he needed.[123]

The cheaper option? The increasing resort to assisted suicide

The number of prescriptions written by doctors in Oregon for lethal drugs for the purpose of assisted suicide as well as the number of resulting deaths from these prescriptions has been steadily increasing since the Death with Dignity Act came into force in 1997. The

---

120   S. James. "Death Drugs Cause Uproar in Oregon". ABC News, Aug. 8 2008. http://abcnews.go.com/Health/story?id=5517492.

121   James. "Death Drugs Cause Uproar".

122   D. Springer. Oregon Offers Terminal Patients Doctor-Assisted Suicide Instead of Medical Care. Fox News July 28, 2008. http://www.foxnews.com/story/2008/07/28/oregon-offers-terminal-patients-doctor-assisted-suicide-instead-medical-care.html

123   Springer. "Oregon Offers Terminal Patients Doctor-Assisted Suicide".

official report from Oregon shows that in the two years from 2013 to 2014 alone, the number of prescriptions rose from 121 to 155, an increase of 28 per cent.[124] The number of deaths also climbed from 73 in 2013 to 105 in 2014.[125] In 1998, the first full year that physician-assisted suicide was legal in Oregon, the number was much lower, with 24 prescriptions handed out and a mere sixteen resulting in death.[126] Between 1998 and 2013, these numbers have been generally increasing, though in some years they have remained constant or even declined slightly.[127] The figures show that assisted suicide is viewed increasingly by physicians and patients as an option when life becomes difficult for individuals and their families. The biggest concern for those who took the lethal drug was not inadequate pain control (31.4 per cent), but rather loss of autonomy (91.4 per cent) and "less ability to engage in activities making life enjoyable" (86.7 per cent). A large percentage (42) said they were partially motivated by the desire not to be a "burden on family, friends/caregivers".[128]

People being put to death because of depression

In 2014 only 2.9 per cent of those who died by lethal overdose under Oregon law had been evaluated by a

---

124   Oregon Public Health Division. Oregon's Death with Dignity Act 2014, p. 1. http://public.health.oregon.gov/ProviderPartnerREsources/ EvaluationResearch/DeathwithDignityAct/Documents/year17.pdf, p. 1

125   Oregon Public Health Division. Oregon's Death with Dignity Act 2014, p. 1.

126   Oregon Public Health Division. Oregon's Death with Dignity Act 2014, p. 1.

127   Oregon Public Health Division. Oregon's Death with Dignity Act 2014, p. 1.

128   Oregon Public Health Division. Oregon's Death with Dignity Act 2014, p. 5.

psychiatrist or a psychologist.[129] This, despite the fact that in a study of 200 terminally-ill cancer patients who expressed a desire to die 59 per cent were likely to have depressive syndromes, compared to only eight per cent who did not express such a desire.[130] Depression, we always need to remember, is a treatable condition. More important, people are in no condition to make decisions about life and death when they are depressed.

Washington

The steady rise in deaths from lethal drugs

Assisted suicide has been legal in Washington since 2009. To date a total of 549 people have been given a lethal prescription.[131] Each year since legalization has seen a significant increase in the number of people requesting prescriptions and in the number who die from lethal drugs. In 2013 the number of prescriptions rose by 43 per cent, to 173, compared to 121 in 2012.[132] The number of patients who were partially motivated by not wanting to be a burden on their family was very high -- 62 per cent of people in both 2012 and 2013 gave this as one of their reasons for requesting a lethal prescription.[133] Opting for

---

129   Oregon Public Health Division. Oregon's Death with Dignity Act 2014, p. 5.

130   H.M. Chochinov, J.J. Clinch, M. Enns, S. Lander, M. Levitt, N. Mowchun, K.G. Wilson. "Desire for Death in the Terminally Ill". Am J Psychiatry Aug 1995; 152; 8:1185-91, p. 1.

131   Washington State Department of Health. Washington State Department of Health 2013 Death with Dignity Act Report Executive Summary, p. 4.

132   Washington State Department of Health. Washington State Department of Health 2013 Death with Dignity Act Report Executive Summary, p. 4.

133   Washington State Department of Health. Washington State Department of Health 2013 Death with Dignity Act Report Executive Summary, p. 4.

assisted suicide is not a decision taken in a vacuum. It is hard to avoid the influence of family members and friends. The sick and elderly can be made to feel guilty for leaning on family and friends when there is an easy way to avoid saddling loved ones with this responsibility.

Conclusion

Euthanasia and assisted suicide are complex issues, hence the title of our book. For many the question is simply one of personal autonomy: no one has the right to prevent me from choosing the time and the manner of my death. This seems to be a stronger consideration in North America than in Europe. In the Netherlands and Belgium it is often the doctor who decides, out of "pity", that euthanasia is the best option for an elderly, severely ill, incompetent or depressed person. In Oregon and Washington, by contrast, many people have the conviction that they are asserting their autonomy by choosing assisted dying. Yet there is troubling evidence in both American states that people are feeling the pressure not to be a burden to their loved ones, or to society, by occupying hospital beds too long, or persisting in expensive medical treatments. There are also signs that people are being told to accept the cheap suicide pill instead of expensive medical treatments. One can foresee that these financial pressures will become more insistent as medical care becomes more expensive.

We are assured that stringent safeguards will protect frail and vulnerable people from being herded towards a death that they do not wish. Yet there is plentiful evidence that the "stringent safeguards" in place both in the Netherlands and Belgium are regularly flouted. True, the number of mentally and physically competent people being put to death without their knowledge or consent had declined recently in the Netherlands, but it is still unacceptably high. In both European countries physicians regularly disregard the law by failing to report when they perform euthanasia or assisted suicide, by failing to consult another physician, and by foisting the administration of lethal injections onto nurses. Some nurses have also taken the law into their own hands by administering injections without a physician's authorization. All in all, the experiences of the Netherlands, Belgium, Oregon and Washington furnish ample reason for concern. Once euthanasia and assisted suicide are legalized we will have opened the door that leads to greater and greater violations of rights, not only of older people, but of people who are not even dying, including infants with disabilities and adolescents suffering from depression.

Chapter 5 *

Why Patients Request Euthanasia and Assisted Suicide

For many people the mention of euthanasia or assisted suicide conjures up the image of a patient suffering unbearable physical pain. Their situation is sometimes compared to that of an animal that has been badly injured, and for which "putting it out of its misery" is seen as a merciful end to its suffering. The analogy is flawed in more than one respect. Not only are human beings radically different from other members of the animal kingdom, we now know a lot more about physical, mental and spiritual pain and how to manage it than we did a few decades ago.

Few terminally-ill patients suffer unbearable pain

It has been determined, for example, that most people who have expressed a clear desire for a hastened death, were, at the time of request in a state of physical pain that was both low and bearable. In a study of terminally-ill cancer patients in New York, the average pain rating on a scale of one to ten was 4.3.[1] This finding calls into question the common understanding of euthanasia and physician-assisted suicide as a compassionate act to end the suffering of a helpless person, where

---

** Chapter 5 written with the assistance of Conor Sweetman.*
1   W. Breitbart, B. Rosenfeld, H. Pessin et al. "Depression, Hopelessness, and Desire for Hastened Death in Terminally Ill Patients with Cancer". JAMA 2000; 284 (22): 2907-11. http://jama.jamanetwork.com/article. aspx?articleid=193350

medication and palliative care are incapable of easing their overwhelming pain. It also raises questions about the underlying reasons behind a patient's request to be euthanized. The aim of this chapter is to explore the mental state of those in such circumstances, identifying and understanding the various reasons why euthanasia and assisted suicide are sought.

Our culture of personal isolation and autonomy

In *The Ethical Canary* Margaret Somerville interprets the rise of public support for euthanasia as symptomatic of a culture of personal isolation, as well as the unparalleled reverence for personal autonomy. With regard to North America's intense individualism, she writes

> The loss of community that individualism breeds can leave us feeling alone and often abandoned when we face death and bereavement. A highly individualistic approach, especially in a society that gives pre-eminence to the values of personal autonomy and self-determination, is likely to encourage the belief that euthanasia is acceptable for those who want it. [2]

The concept of autonomy plays a major role in the average person's view of euthanasia. The political landscape encourages the philosophy of "my body, my choice". We have witnessed this attitude already on issues such as abortion and sexual identity. Those who most strongly support this concept of personal bodily autonomy, especially among society's elite, are

---

2   Margaret Somerville. *The Ethical Canary: Science, Society, and the Human Spirit.* Montreal: McGill-Queen's University Press, 2004, pp. 121-2.

also those who most determinedly proclaim the right to physician-assisted dying.[3] Thus, an authoritative study of patients with ALS and their caregivers revealed that those who most likely to consider assisted suicide were highly-educated caucasian men.[4] In other words, those of higher socio-economic status (as measured by educational level)   preferred this option more than those of lower socio-economic status.[5] In Somerville's estimation, this finding could be a reflection of these individuals' lifelong pursuits of security and control, which at the end of life colour their perspective on death.[6] In another study of patients in Oregon, the researchers found that in the opinion of family members, the strongest factor in their loved ones' requests for physician-assisted suicide was the desire to control the circumstances of their own death, and to die at home by assisted suicide.[7] The Oregon health-care professionals generally agree that patients request euthanasia out of a desire to maintain control and diminish their dependence on others.[8]

Delving deeper into the individualization of North American society, Somerville writes, "a lifetime relationship with a family doctor is largely a relic of

---

3   L. Ganzini, W. Johnston, B. McFarland, S. Tolle, M. Lee. "Attitudes of Patients with Amyotrophic Lateral Sclerosis and Their Care Givers toward Assisted Suicide," NEJM 1998; 339:967-73. http://www.nejm.org/doi/full/10.1056/NEJM199810013391406#t=articleResults

4   Ganzini et al., Attitudes of patients with ALS, pp. 967-73.

5   Ganzini et al., Attitudes of patients with ALS, pp. 967-73.

6   Somerville. *Ethical Canary*, p. 126.

7   L. Ganzini, E.R. Goy, S.K. Dobscha. "Why Oregon patients request assisted death: family members' views." J Gen Intern Med. 2008;23(2):154–157. http://www.ncbi.nlm.nih.gov/pmc/articles/PMC2265314/

8   Ganzini et al. "Why Oregon patients request assisted death", pp. 154-7.

the past, and the isolation that people experience when seeking help from healthcare professionals can be seen as a reflection of the wider isolation that individuals and families encounter in our societies."[9]

This isolation carries into the setting of the hospital, where death is viewed as a purely medical event occurring alone and without solace. Somerville asserts, "death has become sterilized, institutionalized, depersonalized and dehumanized."[10] For these reasons, the demand for euthanasia frequently arises out of culturally-grounded fears and misconceptions that can be addressed through expert counselling. According to the authors of the Oregon study, "the data suggest that when talking with a patient requesting physician assisted-suicide, clinicians should focus on eliciting and addressing worries and apprehension about the future with the goal of reducing anxiety about the dying process."[11]

Assisted suicide will have less to do with personal autonomy and more with external pressures

The most recent official reports from the two American states that have experienced assisted suicide for the longest time show that people are increasingly requesting "assisted dying" for several reasons not connected with personal autonomy or freedom. Prominent among them is the desire not to be a burden on loved ones, or on society as a whole. In Oregon those who expressed a concern that they were a burden on family, friends

---

9   Somerville. *Ethical Canary,* p. 120

10   Somerville. *Ethical Canary,* p. 120

11   Ganzini et al. "Why Oregon patients request assisted death", pp. 154–7.

or caregivers rose from 40 to 42 per cent between 1998-2013 and 2014. Those worried about but not actually experiencing inadequate pain control rose from 24 to 33 per cent. Those with financial worries about their treatments declined from 22 to five per cent. Other concerns were "losing autonomy" (96 per cent), being less able to engage in activities making life enjoyable (91 per cent), and loss of dignity (75 per cent).[12]

In Washington in 2014 89 per cent of those who requested assisted suicide said they were concerned about loss of autonomy, 79 per cent about loss of dignity, and 94 per cent about loss of the ability to participate in activities that make life enjoyable.[13] However, a surprising 59 per cent were concerned about being a burden to family, friends or caregivers, 51 per cent about losing control of bodily functions, 41 per cent about potential future inadequate pain control, and eight per cent about financial concerns.[14]

Those who support assisted suicide in theory rarely want it for themselves

Given our underlying cultural bias in favour of personal autonomy and freedom, it is little wonder that euthanasia and assisted suicide have generated so much public support. However, there is a notable discrepancy between supporting euthanasia in principle, and

---

12   Oregon's Death with Dignity Act – 2014, p. 5. https://public.health.oregon.gov/ProviderPartnerResources/EvaluationResearch/DeathwithDignityAct/Pages/ar-index.aspx

13   Washington State Department of Health 2014 Death with Dignity Act Report, p. 1. http://www.doh.wa.gov/YouandYourFamily/IllnessandDisease/DeathwithDignityAct

14   Washington State Department of Health 2014 Death with Dignity Act Report, p. 7.

supporting its actual implementation. A large study of terminally-ill patients across the U.S. showed that a total of 60.2 per cent supported euthanasia or physician-assisted suicide in a hypothetical situation, but only 10.6 per cent said that they would seriously consider it for themselves.[15] The reluctance to ask for euthanasia, even though the subjects were near the point of death, and despite having expressed support in theory for the idea, is revealing. The apparently strong support for euthanasia and assisted suicide nearly evaporates when it is comes down to the issue of a person's own life. In both studies only a small minority of terminally-ill patients were prepared to consider euthanasia for themselves, and even fewer took concrete action, such as requesting assistance in dying from physicians.[16] According to the study on ALS patients, these findings support the notion that a patient is often psychologically comforted by the knowledge that they have the option to take a lethal dose of drugs if they so desire.[17] Perhaps less dangerous options than easy access to suicide could be found to give comparable psychological comfort to these patients.

The motives of those who do request assisted suicide

Now let us examine the reasons why those who actually request euthanasia do so. Here again, recent research

---

15   E. Emanuel, D. Fairclough, L. Emanuel. "Attitudes and Desires Related to Euthanasia and Physician-Assisted Suicide Among Terminally Ill Patients and Their Caregivers." JAMA. 2000;284 (19):2460-8. http://jama.jamanetwork.com/article.aspx?articleid=193281.
16   Ganzini et al. "Attitudes of Patients with Amyotrophic Lateral Sclerosis", pp. 967-73.
17   Ganzini et al. "Attitudes of Patients with Amyotrophic Lateral Sclerosis", pp. 967-73.

has surprises for us. The importance of physical pain, which often occupies centre stage in the conversation, has been found to be far less than used to be thought. When patients in Oregon who supported euthanasia rated their current pain, they placed it no higher than two on a scale of one to five.[18] A study of cancer patients in New York, revealed that 78 per cent reported their pain during the preceding two weeks as averaging 4.3 on a scale of one to ten, reflecting mild to moderate pain.[19] It was also found in the large American study that those experiencing moderate or severe pain were not more likely to support euthanasia or assisted suicide based merely on the basis of pain alone.[20] Even a patient who is enduring considerable pain, of an intensity that is commonly viewed as justifying euthanasia, is on average no more favourable to euthanasia than the one who experiences low to moderate pain. Therefore, although physical pain may be a contributing factor to the desire for hastened death, physical pain is not in itself the driving motivation.

It is the fear of future pain that spurs the demand for assisted suicide

Far more than immediate pain being the underlying reason, there is a pervasive fear of *future* physical

---

18   L. Ganzini, E.R. Goy, S.K. Dobscha. "Why Oregon patients request assisted death: family members' views." J Gen Intern Med. 2008;23(2):154–157. http://www.ncbi.nlm.nih.gov/pmc/articles/PMC2265314/

19   W.Breitbart, B. Rosenfeld, H. Pessin, et al. "Depression, Hopelessness, and Desire for Hastened Death in Terminally Ill Patients With Cancer." JAMA 2000;284 (22):2907-11. http://jama.jamanetwork.com/article.aspx?articleid=193350.

20   Emanuel et al. "Attitudes and Desires Related to Euthanasia and Physician-Assisted Suicide", pp. 2460-68. http://jama.jamanetwork.com/article.aspx?articleid=193281

suffering, spurred mostly by the expectation that palliative care will be unable to meet fully the need for pain management.[21] In other words the fear of future pain looms much larger in the patient's mind than present pain as a reason for requesting assistant suicide. This future-oriented fear spurs the desire for euthanasia, which otherwise is wavering and unstable. It was found in a study by Chochinov and colleagues that 40 per cent of those who say that they would potentially ask for a lethal dose of drugs admit they would only have wanted it in the past or at some future time, but not in the present.[22] When questioned further about why they would have asked for assisted suicide earlier, many replied that they had been caught in a time of seemingly unbearable psychological and physical pain and distress and sought a way to end it. However, with the passage of time, the intensity of distress waned, and they arrived at their present state without the desire to commit assisted suicide.[23] This finding is corroborated in the study ALS patients, which showed that a large portion of them said they would consider assisted suicide, and 44 per cent said they would request a prescription for a lethal dose of medication from a physician if it were a legal option.[24] However, only one patient stated that he would take the medicine immediately. Those who were

---

21   L. Ganzini, E.R. Goy, S.K. Dobscha. "Why Oregon patients request assisted death: family members' views." J Gen Intern Med. 2008;23(2):154–7. http://www.ncbi.nlm.nih.gov/pmc/articles/ PMC2265314/

22   K. Wilson, H. Chochinov, C. McPherson, M. Skirko, P. Allard, S. Chary, J. Clinch, et al. "Desire for euthanasia or physician-assisted suicide in palliative cancer care." Health Psychology 2007;26(3): 314-23. PsycArticles, EBSCOhost.

23   Wilson et al. "Desire for euthanasia", pp. 314-23.

24   Ganzini et al. "Attitudes of Patients with ALS", pp. 967-73.

interviewed and desired euthanasia presently were the outliers -- the majority would not have initiated such a request at the time of the interview.

Depressed people are more likely to demand assisted suicide

We also know that most of the key determinants of interest in euthanasia and physician-assisted suicide have to do, not with physical symptoms, but psychological distress and care needs.[25] The mental distress of those who desire hastened death is usually caused in part by the presence of clinical depression and a sense of hopelessness.[26] The study of cancer patients in New York reveals the extreme relevance of depression as a factor.

> Of fifteen patients who met criteria for a major depressive episode, seven were classified as having a high desire for hastened death and eight were not. Conversely, among the 74 patients who were not depressed, nine had a high desire for hastened death while 65 did not. Thus, patients with a major depression were four times more likely to have high desire for hastened death.[27]

This contradicts the notion that clinical depression is not a pervasive factor in the desire for euthanasia.

---

25   Emanuel. "Attitudes and Desires Related to Euthanasia and Physician-Assisted Suicide", pp. 2460-8.
26   Breitbart. "Depression, Hopelessness, and Desire for Hastened Death", pp. 2907-11.
27   Breitbart. "Depression, Hopelessness, and Desire for Hastened Death", pp. 2907-11.

People's demand for euthanasia is often transitory

Other researchers emphasize that "because euthanasia and PAS are irreversible actions, longitudinal assessments of patients' attitudes and preferences are important."[28] They are convinced that the desire for euthanasia and assisted suicide is quite unstable in their patients. In fact, "about half the terminally-ill patients interested in euthanasia or assisted suicide changed their minds, and terminally ill patients who had not previously considered these interventions began to do so..."[29] They thus advise physicians who receive requests for euthanasia or assisted suicide to recognize their volatility and not take such requests as settled views. Rather they should evaluate patients for depression and unrelieved dysthymia, explaining depressive mood swings.[30] Buttressing the concept of wavering mindsets behind the desire for euthanasia, another research team involving H. Chochinov showed that for the individuals who desired euthanasia, "Pain and symptoms, including mental stress, were reported as the most important reasons for the desire to die."[31] In addition 43.5 per cent of patients reported experiences of uncontrolled pain, as well as generalized episodes of suffering and psychological considerations including mental stress, low quality of life and even the shock of receiving a terminal prognosis.[32] What is

---

28   Emanuel. "Attitudes and Desires Related to Euthanasia and Physician-Assisted Suicide", pp. 2460-8.
29   Emanuel. "Attitudes and Desires Related to Euthanasia and Physician-Assisted Suicide", pp. 2460-8.
30   Emanuel. "Attitudes and Desires Related to Euthanasia and Physician-Assisted Suicide", pp. 2460-8.
31   Wilson et al. "Desire for euthanasia , pp. 314-23.
32   Wilson et al. "Desire for euthanasia", pp. 314-23.

most significant, however, is that their acute suffering turned out to be controllable, and their desire for death was transitory. More and more we are learning that people continue to be driven to request euthanasia by symptoms that are potentially treatable.

Hopelessness as another motive

Yet another factor in the desire for euthanasia is hopelessness. How does hopelessness differ from depression? Unlike clinical depression, it is characterized by a pessimistic cognitive style rather than an assessment of one's poor prognosis.[33] It has been defined as "a way of thinking in which negative expectations about the future are pervasive."[34] One statement that the patients were asked to agree or disagree with in order to locate their place on the Beck Hopelessness Scale was "I look forward to the future with hope and enthusiasm." Of those who agreed, 84 per cent would not consider assisted suicide, since they felt no need to hasten the end of a hopeless life in which there was no purpose in waking up for another day.[35] This finding reveals the radical difference in the mindset of patients under similar objective circumstances, one group having peace about the future, the other not.

What we can perceive through this examination of various studies on the motivation for seeking euthanasia, is the clear contrast between attitudes and practices, between the reasons why people find euthanasia

---

33 Breitbart. "Depression, Hopelessness, and Desire for Hastened Death", pp. 2907-11.

34 Ganzini et al. "Attitudes of Patients with ALS", pp. 967-73.

35 Ganzini et al. "Attitudes of Patients with ALS", pp. 967-73.

and assisted suicide acceptable, and the reasons why very few will opt for it. The reasons why people find it acceptable in principle have to do predominantly with pain, while the main factor motivating their *actual* willingness to accept it for themselves, is most often fear of the future, depression and hopelessness.

Religious faith as a factor

The presence of religious faith may be correlated with a much lower frequency of major depression than among those without religious faith.[36] In an important American study those who favoured legalization of euthanasia and physician-assisted suicide, and who desired a hastened death had lower religiosity and were more likely to have prescriptions for benzodiazepine (anti-anxiety) and neuroleptic (anti-psychotic) medications. About 40 per cent of them met diagnostic criteria for major depression – more than double the prevalence of major depression among those who did *not* desire hastened death. They also reported much higher levels of anxiety, hopelessness and dissatisfaction with life. These are objective indications of their greater distress. It was evidently this distress that prompted their physicians to prescribe the drugs to ease their suffering.[37]

The irrevocable character of assisted suicide

Although euthanasia and assisted suicide have been "covered by a medical cloak"[38] in Margaret Somerville's

---

36   Wilson et al. "Desire for euthanasia", pp. 314-23.
37   Wilson et al. "Desire for euthanasia", pp. 314-23.
38   Somerville, *Ethical Canary*, p.125.

words, the action of ending a life intentionally, whether by suicide, or the killing of another person by homicide, is a dramatic, irreversible action. The consequences should therefore be fully grasped. The drastic, irrevocable character of assisted suicide has especially been ignored in North America, thanks to our tendency to envision it as applying only to extremely elderly invalids who are tormented by untreatable pain. We do not imagine that it may soon be possible for people with treatable depression to choose assisted suicide. We cannot foresee the day when it will no longer be permitted to take drastic measures against suicide, such as suicide awareness campaigns, mandatory counselling, suicide prevention hotlines, emergency medical treatment for those who have harmed themselves in a suicide attempt, and even forcible intervention to stop someone from killing themself.

If depression is a significant cause of both euthanasia and suicide, the distinction between the two will be increasingly blurred and preventive measures will come to be seen as increasingly useless or even counter-productive. We see this danger illustrated clearly in the case of the 24-year-old Belgian woman who was approved for euthanasia merely because she had experienced suicidal thoughts since her childhood. What this means is that in Belgium lethal injections are now available to young people suffering from treatable depression.[39] In the words of Alex Schadenberg, "once you allow killing for one reason, there are many reasons people might want to die. The only question

---

39   Butts C, "Belgium's 'sad path' for assisted suicide" *One News Network*, July 22, 2015, http://www.onenewsnow.com/pro-life/2015/07/22/belgiums-sad-path-for-assisted-suicide

is what are we going to say yes or no to. In Belgium they've gone far down that road. It is better never to enter that road"[40]

Conclusion

In this chapter we have seen that there are a variety of reasons why people request assisted suicide. In the U.S. the loss of personal autonomy appears to be a paramount concern, along with loss of dignity, and the inability to engage in life's enjoyable activities. Elsewhere clinical depression—a common, but treatable psychological phenomenon—is perhaps the most frequent. The desire not to be a burden is another. The anticipation of pain, rather than pain itself is another. Fear of suffering and the unknown is another. Feelings of hopelessness and meaninglessness are another. All these latter reasons have very little to do with the assertion of personal autonomy, and a great deal to do with loneliness and the conviction that no one cares. What can be done, apart from the offer of "assisted dying", to bring compassionate care to those in need? That is the subject of Chapter Six.

---

40   Quoted in Butts. "Belgium's 'sad path'".

Chapter 6 *

Quality of Life with Palliative Care
Not Euthanasia

Let us now turn to the alternatives that must be available for all citizens of Canada in light of the revolutionary ruling of our Supreme Court to legalize euthanasia and physician-assisted suicide. It must never be forgotten that this ruling was handed down in defiance of the clearly- expressed and considered decision by Parliament in 2010 to reject overwhelmingly a bill that would have decriminalized euthanasia and assisted suicide.[1] At the time many believed this vote demonstrated to the rest of the world Canada's compassion and concern for quality end-of-life care, as well as a commitment to protecting our most vulnerable citizens against unwanted killing.

Following this vote, five federal parliamentarians founded the "Parliamentary Committee on Palliative and Compassionate Care" (PCPCC). Close to 60 MPs and former MPs from all parties publicly or quietly supported the committee's work. Many individuals, organizations and groups provided input at their own expense to make the committee's hearings possible. Several of the participants were there on behalf of vulnerable Canadians.

Chapter 6 written with the assistance of Lisa Hamilton.

1   http://www.cbc.ca/news/canada/assisted-suicide-voted-down-by-mps-1.910839 (April 21, 2010).

Care for the vulnerable

In November 2011 the committee published *Not to be Forgotten: Care of Vulnerable Canadians*.[2] This document comprises three sections:

- Part 1: Palliative and End-of-Life Care

- Part 2: Suicide Prevention

- Part 3: Elder Abuse: Canada's Hidden Crime

In spite of the remarkable content in this document the government has not yet taken any action. Even the recommendation to re-establish a national Palliative Care Secretariat has been neglected. If it were adopted it would make possible the development and implementation of a National Palliative and End-of-Life Care Strategy for Canada.

Following the British example, Dr Balfour Mount introduced palliative care in Canada at Montreal's Royal Victoria Hospital. His shining example has been widely imitated across Canada, but much more remains to be done for patients suffering pain and other noxious but manageable symptoms associated with life-threatening, progressive and terminal disease. The principles and practices of good hospice palliative care are already well developed and practised in Canada. They have made it abundantly clear that there is no need for anyone in this country to die in pain, loneliness and anxiety, or bereft of dignity. It is urgent

2   Harold Albrecht, Joseph Comartin, Frank Valeriote, Kelly Block, Francis Scarpaleggia. *Not to be Forgotten: Care of Vulnerable Canadians.* Ottawa: Parliamentary Committee on Palliative and Compassionate Care, 2011.

that hospice palliative care services be available for all Canadians regardless of age or disease, and whether their illness is physical or emotional. People of all ages must be eligible: babies, toddlers, adolescents, adults and the elderly. To do less is to abandon our social, ethical and moral responsibilities when our fellow citizens are at their most vulnerable. As well, for those of us in healthcare professions, to abandon them in their time of need would be to betray our professional responsibilities, duties and standards of practice.

The eruption of widespread demand for the decriminalization of euthanasia and assisted suicide in recent years tells us that our healthcare system has failed people when they are at their sickest and most vulnerable. It makes no sense to think that death based on the notion of "radical autonomy" can be a rational alternative to improving quality of life through palliative care. Radical autonomists, with their nearly exclusive focus on "self," run the danger of hurting many others besides themselves.

An imposition on doctors, nurses and institutions

Even when taking the focus away from the patients on the receiving end of this new "death service," we must consider the implications for our doctors, nurses, long-term care institutions and hospitals. Inflicting death on another human being is the ultimate act of violence and all citizens need to pose this question to themselves: "How dare we ask our doctors (and nurses) to kill us?" In our opinion, doctors who opt for euthanasia will soon lose the trust they presently enjoy from their patients and the general public. The same will hold true for any acute and long-term care institution that permits persons to be put to death under its roof.

What of those who administer the lethal dose? Will they experience psychic trauma or existential/spiritual crises, moral distress or moral disengagement as a result? Will they develop Post Traumatic Stress Disorder (PTSD) with its inherent anxiety and depression? What type of collateral psychic harm will be wreaked on others working on the inter-professional team, not to mention patients and their families?

Professional nurses

Another critical issue raised by the Supreme Court's ruling is not even mentioned in their document. It concerns the role of professional nurses. They are the ones who are at the bedside for the longest period of time of any healthcare provider in acute, long-term and community-care settings. Inevitably they will become assistants and collaborators in any type of inflicted death. How will engaging in the act of causing death align with regulatory requirements and standards of nursing practice? The Canadian Nurses Association (CNA) Code of Ethics requires that: "In all practice settings, nurses work to relieve pain and suffering, including appropriate and effective symptom and pain management, to live with dignity."[3] The ethical obligation is clearly about preserving life; there is no reference to hastening or causing death. Since the nursing role is historically and currently significant, it is

---

3   Canadian Nurses Association. *Code of Ethics.* (June 2008). http://cna-aiic.ca/~/media/cna/page-content/pdf-en/code_of_ethics_2008_e.pdf

essential that nurses also have the right of conscientious objection when asked to hasten the death of a patient.

Currently a majority of physicians who belong to the Canadian Society of Palliative Care Physicians (CSPCP) are refusing to perform the death procedures of euthanasia and assisted suicide.[4] Furthermore, the Canadian Christian Medical and Dental Society (CMDS)[5] is challenging the College of Physicians and Surgeons of Ontario (CPSO) regarding their draft policy entitled: "Professional Obligations and Human Rights."[6] This policy locks physicians with a religious or conscientious objection into the intolerable position of having to refer patients requesting euthanasia or assisted suicide to another physician who will do the euthanizing. To refer for assisted suicide is to be complicit in the act. No physician who has a conscientious or religious objection to the practice could possibly refer a patient to a doctor who is willing to carry it out. The CPSO draft policy is fundamentally discriminatory and prejudicial against doctors and nurses who hold life-affirming values and beliefs, or faith-based principles. It is unacceptable for our professional leaders to dictate any type of participation in euthanasia or assisted suicide, including referrals. Referrals equal complicity. Suppose female genital

---

4   Canadian Society of Palliative Care Physicians. *Position Statement Following Supreme Court Judgment re: Carter* (February 12, 2015) http://www.cspcp.ca/wp-content/uploads/2014/10/CSPCP-Position-Following-SCC-Judgment-12-Feb-2015.pdf

5   Christian Medical Dental Society - Canada. http://www.cmdscanada.org/ConscienceProtection.aspx

6   College of Physicians and Surgeons of Ontario. *Professional Obligations and Human Rights.* http://policyconsult.cpso.on.ca/wp-content/uploads/2014/12/Draft-Professional-Obligations-and-Human-Rights.pdf

mutilation were a legally provided "health service", would we then require physicians with a religious or conscientious objection to genital mutilation to refer patients for this "service?" We should recall that freedom of religion and conscience is entirely protected and guarded by our Canadian Charter of Rights and Freedoms. No physician, nurse or healthcare institution can be coerced into violating their beliefs by participating in the killing of patients.

The Supreme Court of Canada's ruling creates a new social disorder which we label "death management/death care" since euthanasia and assisted suicide deal only with the process of causing an individual's death. These services should not be associated with hospice palliative care, which is a medical and nursing specialty or with healthcare in general. Death management or death care must be a stand-alone entity or service.

It ought to be a matter of public shame that approximately 70 to 80 per cent of Canadians have no access to palliative care and these services exist only sporadically and mainly in urban centres.[7] Added to this is the lack of palliative care in our long-term care facilities because of limited resources and lack of knowledge. Furthermore, our federal and provincial governments have failed to support the development of this specialty and in fact have hindered it by denial of funds. Also, we have failed to educate our medical and nursing students in the principles and practices

---

7   H.M. Chochinov. "We have a right to die but not to quality palliative care." *The Province.* Feb. 24, 2015. http:\\www.the province. com/story print.html?id=10837975&sponsor=true

of palliative care, and the importance of excellence in end-of-life care. We are failing to provide ongoing education for our current complement of doctors and nurses and most unfortunately, we have failed to educate the Canadian public in the meaning, purpose and help that can be derived from patient-family referral to this specialty care. Hospice palliative care must be available for every Canadian since it is by far the best alternative to euthanasia and physician-assisted suicide.

Vulnerable groups

How will we protect those individuals at high risk for abuse in this new social disorder that we choose to label "death management?" These include the elderly, especially women who continue to suffer from a lingering culture of misogyny; persons with physical and emotional disabilities; patients with chronic or life-threatening diseases; victims of domestic violence where there is a power imbalance; individuals experiencing suicidal ideation as it relates to distressing life events; cultural and ethnic groups including our First Nations, Métis and Inuit people. At risk is another group: those waiting in acute-care beds for openings in long-term care facilities. They are often stigmatized and referred to as "bed blockers."

With regard to domestic violence and "power imbalance" one of the authors has direct knowledge of the so-called "suicide" of three different women at the behest of their husbands. The husbands prevailed upon their wives to overdose themselves in order to be rid of them and safely carry on with new, already-involved partners. Once the practice of euthanasia and assisted suicide has become entrenched in Canadian society, it is not clear how such an abuse pattern will be detected. It is often hard to know what is going on at home.

The features of good palliative care

What kind of a difference could an adequate program of palliative care make in the lives of Canadians facing advanced illness, a life-threatening diagnosis, or terminal disease?

The World Health Organization (WHO) defines palliative care as: "an approach that improves the quality of life of patients and their families facing the problems associated with life-threatening illness, through the prevention and relief of suffering by means of early identification and impeccable assessment and treatment of pain and other problems physical, psychosocial and spiritual."[8] WHO elaborates on the underlying principles of good palliative care as follows: It

- provides relief from pain and other distressing symptoms

- affirms life and regards dying as a normal process

- intends neither to hasten nor postpone death

- integrates the psychological and spiritual

---

8   World Health Organization. *WHO Definition of Palliative Care.* http://www.who.int/cancer/palliative/definition/en/

aspects of palliative care

- offers a support system to help patients live as actively as possible until death

- offers a support system to help the family cope during the patient's illness and in their own bereavement

- uses a team approach to address the needs of patients and their families, including bereavement counselling, if indicated

- will enhance quality of life and may also positively influence the course of illness

- is applicable early in the course of illness, in conjunction with other therapies that are intended to prolong life, such as chemotherapy or radiation therapy and includes those investigations needed to understand and manage better distressing clinical complications.

In the same manner, the WHO has defined palliative care for children. Included in the principles is that palliative care begins when the illness is diagnosed and continues regardless of whether or not a child receives treatment directed at the disease.[9]

The Canadian Hospice Palliative Care Association (CHPCA), the national association providing leadership in hospice palliative care in Canada, describes palliative

---

9   World Health Organization. *WHO Definition of Palliative Care.* http://www.who.int/cancer/palliative/definition/en/

care as, "whole-person health care that aims to relieve suffering and improve the quality of living and dying. The purpose of hospice palliative care is to help patients and families: address physical, psychological, social, spiritual and practical issues, and their associated expectations, needs, hopes and fears; prepare for and manage the dying process; and cope with loss and grief during the illness and bereavement. Hospice palliative care is appropriate for any patient or family living with, or at risk of developing, a life-limiting illness due to any diagnosis, with any prognosis, regardless of age, and at any time they have unmet expectations and/or needs, and are prepared to accept care."[10]

"Palliative care" does not have to mean you are "terminally ill"

In addition CHPCA makes the point that the inter-professional team of palliative-care specialists must be involved much earlier on the life-threatening disease trajectory. If every program had focused their sights earlier on this more comprehensive definition, vision and principles, we could potentially have had more public understanding, federal and provincial government support, educational backing and much less fear surrounding the term "hospice palliative care". We also note that "hospice" and "palliative care" are used interchangeably, and neither necessarily implies terminal illness. Early on in the hospice palliative care movement, there was an inclusive societal interpretation of the management of terminal illness with its major focus on death and dying. If this

---

10   Canadian Hospice Palliative Association. *Mission and Vision.* http://www.chpca.net/about-us/mission-and-vision.aspx

narrower focus can be broadened, we suggest that it will foster increased referrals, expansion of programs, research and further development of this much needed specialty. This is because there will be a greater focus on quality of life while the person is living and they will not immediately be labelled "terminal."

The experience of a palliative-care hospice in South-western Ontario

At its inception in the 1980s the Hospice of Windsor and Essex County, Inc. took the broad interpretation of hospice palliative care and encouraged referral at a much earlier stage of illness inclusive of diagnosis. Restricting the criteria for patient population to the last six months was too rigid both operationally and philosophically. As Jean Echlin wrote,

> In some palliative-care situations, we have noted a "renewed will to live syndrome" enabling a better outlook and enhanced quality of life. Effective management of symptoms has resulted in resumption of active treatment. Therefore, as healthcare providers, we must re-examine the tendency to label people dying or terminal.[11]

Supporting this approach, we have Dr. Cicely Saunders' comments on the relationship between active palliative care and terminal care: "the aims of the two are not mutually exclusive, and effective control of symptoms may accompany or revive the prospect of

---

11   Jean Echlin ,"Palliative Care and the Neuman Model", in Betty Neuman, *Neuman Systems Model: Application to Nursing Education and Practice.* Norwalk, CT: Appleton-Century-Crofts, 1982, p. 259.

further treatment."[12] What are the outcomes? Answer: enhanced quality of life supported by hospice palliative care and the resumption of acute care treatment. In this light the provision of broadly-based palliative care appears much more life- and dignity-enhancing than an approach that focuses chiefly on preparing the patient for death.

Palliative care should be introduced from the initial diagnosis of a life-threatening disease, not when the patient has already transitioned to the terminal stage. This is especially important when pain and symptom management are significant problems. One of the biggest issues has been referrals that come too late.

Robert S.'s story

The following story illustrates the point. Robert S. was only 39. He had a wife and four children under the age of thirteen. Diagnosed with metastatic adenocarcinoma of the stomach, Rob was angry, not only at his diagnosis but also at the idea of being referred to as "terminal." At the time much of the media had labelled the palliative care team as the "death squad!" Thus the public and patients associated the words hospice palliative care with nothing other than terminal illness, dying and death.

From his hospital bed Rob pointed to the communications desk and insisted that his nurse "go and tell those people out there 'DO NOT LABEL ME

---

12   Cicely Saunders, *The Management of Terminal Disease*. London: Edward Arnold, 1979. pp. 8-9.

TERMINAL!' Give me a measure of hope and speak to my living. I will tell you when I am ready to discuss my dying!" It often happens that people labelled "terminal" live for months or even years. Predicting the date of a person's death can act as a self-fulfilling prophecy that may hinder living longer.

Mrs. T.'s story

Here is another example of a terminal label stuck on much too soon. Mrs. T. was diagnosed with "end-stage" or "terminal" pancreatic cancer five years ago. With a unique combination of chemotherapy and excellence in symptom management, she has lived five years beyond her initial diagnosis with what she describes as "great quality of life despite the 'ups' and 'downs.'" Part of the reason why this was so successful was the collaboration between the local cancer centre and palliative-care programs. The provision of quality palliative care can extend life-expectancy especially when combined with excellent pain and symptom management.[13]

Relating this back to Rob, he too lived for another year-and-a-half, and with effective pain and symptom management he accomplished many things that loomed in importance for him. Rob noted that he could not have done this "without the support of hospice

---

13   J.Temmel, et al., "Early Palliative Care for Patients with Metastatic Non-Small-Cell Lung Cancer." NEJM 2010; 363(8): pp. 733-42; J.A. Greer et al., "Effect of Early Palliative Care on Chemotherapy Use and End-of-Life Care in Patients with Metastatic with Non-Small-Cell Lung Cancer." Journal of Clinical Oncology 2012; 30(4):; pp. 394-400; M. Bakitaset al., "The Project ENABLE ll Randomized Controlled Trial to Improve Palliative Care for Patients with Advanced Cancer." JAMA 2009: 302(7): pp. 741-9.

palliative care in addition to the active chemotherapy and radiotherapy" that he was receiving. This was made possible by the full support that his palliative-care team received from the medical oncologists of the Regional Cancer Centre.

Historically, hospice or palliative care focused on the person afflicted with terminal cancer. Today palliative-care principles and practices are being applied to many other chronic and life-limiting diseases such as renal failure (kidney), cardiovascular diseases (heart and stroke), motor neuron illness such as Amyotrophic Lateral Sclerosis (ALS) also known as Lou-Gehrig's Disease, and Multiple Sclerosis (MS). That is why we must encourage the WHO and CHPCA's definitions for palliative care so that people are less inclined to turn away from the services available to them simply because they have learned to associate them with dying and death.

Rob's situation also illustrates how adding euthanasia and assisted suicide to the hospice palliative care menu of programs can be disastrous for individuals and their families. Rob's plea highlights the reason why so many people have avoided hospice palliative care over these years: because of a near-universal fear of death and the stigma associated with the terms hospice and palliative care. Paradoxically, society today has become fixated on death, almost enamoured with it. We seek total control over the experience. Yet this morbid need to control death is fuelled by fear.

Good palliative care equals quality of life

Hospice palliative care distinctively values quality of life during life-threatening or advanced illness as well as end-of-life. It speaks to excellence in the management of physical, social, emotional and spiritual pain and discomfort. This is the original concept of "total pain" defined by Dr. (Dame) Cicely Saunders at St. Christopher's Hospice, London, England.[14] Adding euthanasia and assisted suicide to the palliative care continuum is morally objectionable and unacceptable since these procedures focus only on death management and death.

To paraphrase Dr. Saunders, many chronic diseases possess the capacity to shut a person or individual off almost completely from those around, including society at large. Constant nausea, intractable dyspnea (shortness of breath), or pain accompany many chronic diseases. A patient may feel like a prisoner in a kind of solitary confinement.[15] Palliative care as a medical specialty has challenged and overcome this subjective feeling of isolation and abandonment.

Barbara L.'s story

Another story that illustrates the need for and positive effects of early referral to a hospice palliative care program is Barbara L. She was a 37-year-old wife and mother of two sons aged five and seven. As a professional psychotherapist she had a keen awareness of her own body and its functions. Barbara

---

14   Cicely Saunders. *Management of Terminal Disease*. London: Edward Arnold, 1979, pp.194-5.

15   Saunders, *Management of Terminal Disease*, p. 9.

was initially diagnosed with stage IV estrogen receptor negative breast cancer. She was admitted to hospital with metastatic lesions in her lower spine and a serious lymphedema (swelling) of her left arm. Radiation therapy called "spot-radiation" helped with the spinal pain for another six weeks. However, other lesions in the spinal vertebrae developed, causing increasing pain intensity. This was described by Barbara as being "ten **plus plus plus**" out of ten on a Verbal Analog Scale (VAS). The scale ranges from zero to ten, zero being no pain, ten being the worst pain possible.

Intensive pain management

Barb desperately wanted to go home for Christmas. She had finished several rounds of chemotherapy and had undergone maximum doses of radiation. Intensive methods of pain management associated with palliative care were put in place. The use of opiates/opioids (narcotics) is standard treatment in any palliative-care setting. With Barb, this included the use of a pain pump connected to a venous reservoir. This allowed for a constant level of pain-relieving morphine to be present in her bloodstream. Her dosage of morphine was carefully titrated (meaning that the concentration of narcotic was carefully moved up or down) upwards. The method for this generally involves increasing the dose by 25 to 50 per cent of the original dose according to regulations until maximum pain relief is experienced without sedation. Before she was able to regain appropriate mobility, Barb was receiving 1,080 mg (milligrams) of morphine every 24 hours. This represented a constant hourly rate of 45 mg. A typical maximum dosage recommendation for morphine varies depending on age, body size and other variables; however, 2.5 to 10 mg every four hours for a total of 15 to 60 mg daily is a common therapeutic range.

The example of Barbara's agonizing pain illustrates the need for clinical practitioners to be ready to venture outside normal dosage ranges when providing palliative care. It is known to healthcare professionals that the common side effects to be monitored for narcotic use are changes in neurological status (for example, the patient is difficult to rouse) and depression of respiratory (breathing) rate. Barb's neurological state (awake and alert) remained unaffected, her breathing pattern was completely normal, and she was able to regain her mobility. She even designed and made small fabric pouches to hold the pain pump that matched her clothing. Barbara went home and was able to go out for dinner on Christmas Day. Most importantly she was able to talk to her husband and sons about what she hoped for them, her spiritual beliefs, and how she would love them even after her death.

Yet Barbara at first adamantly refused to have any interaction with hospice palliative care believing it was only about death and dying. She asserted, "I am not terminal, I am not dying right now, don't let those hospice people near me!" After much discussion and clarification on the principles and practice of hospice palliative care, she came to understand that the team was focused on quality of life not just on death and dying. Another important part of Barbara's story will amaze those concerned about addiction and alarmed over the possibility of morphine causing death. Prior to her death she was able to receive additional "spot radiation" to the spinal lesions. The result was her ability to reduce the morphine level in her pain pump from 1,048 mg in 24 hours to 120mg in 24 hours or 5 mg per hour.

Robert and Barbara shared a common outlook, similar to many who fear the words hospice and palliative solely because of a lack of public understanding of the real depth, breadth and meaning of hospice palliative care. If we referred to quality of life in *advanced* and *life-threatening illness*, rather than *terminal* illness, we would gain a real advantage in teaching the true meaning and value behind hospice palliative care. Associating hospice palliative care solely with the end of life may also explain why healthcare professionals are often reluctant to discuss this option with their patients.

Jean Echlin, a palliative care nursing consultant has had the privilege and honour of walking life's journey with hundreds of individuals and their families in Southwestern Ontario. The fear of pain and suffering over how dying will happen, produces high levels of anxiety. As individuals and their loved ones looked for guidance and relief from this daunting anxiety, a trust relationship with Echlin was established in an astoundingly short period of time. Over the course of her 36-year career, not a single patient ever asked for euthanasia. She has been asked for help within Saunders' framework of "total pain" including physical, emotional, social and spiritual suffering, but never did any of her patients mention practices outside of these domains. She has personally witnessed the transformative effect of excellence in the management of physical symptoms. Once the symptoms were taken care of as the first priority, patients felt able to redirect their attention to the other facets of their life they felt needed attention.

The negative example of Holland: the abandonment of palliative care

According to Hugh Matthews, writing in the *British Medical Journal*, euthanasia in the Netherlands "is proving detrimental to the practice of medicine and is usually avoidable."[16] He cites the opinions of Dr. Ben Zylicz, a Dutch palliative-care physician who pointed out that there were only 70 specialist palliative care beds in the whole country, compared to many thousands in Britain, which is a country only four-times larger. He was certain that this shortage of beds was one reason why doctors and patients resorted to euthanasia. Dr. Zylicz further reports that patients with a terminal illness are typically discharged to their general practitioner. In the virtual absence of palliative-care medicine, general practitioners feel that they have no recourse except euthanasia to stop their patients' suffering. In the same article, Professor Lord McColl, a member of the UK's House of Lords' Select Committee on Euthanasia made a visit to the Netherlands and concluded, "our visit convinced me that euthanasia is impossible to police and will be abused."[17]

The principles and practice of palliative care

In the clinical and volunteer development of the mission statement of philosophy, goals, standards and objectives originally devised for the Hospice of Windsor, Echlin employed a number of theoretical and conceptual models in order to maintain academic

---

16   H. Matthews. "Better Palliative Care Could Cut Euthanasia."
BMJ 1998; 317 (7173): p.1613.
17   Matthews, "Better Palliative Care," p. 1613.

credibility and sound ethical philosophy for professional staff, volunteers and nursing students. Among them were Margaret Newman's "Concept of Wellness in Chronic Illness;" Martha Rogers' "Unitary Man;" Betty Neuman's "The Neuman Systems Model: Application to Nursing Education and Practice;" Leininger's "Transcultural Nursing;" Martin Seligman's "Theory of Learned Helplessness;" Avery Wiseman's "Concept of Hope and Effect on Quality of Life;" Hans Selye's "Stress Adaptation Model;" and Victor Frankl's "Man's Search for Meaning." All of these frameworks and models support the principles and practice of palliative care. They and the statements Echlin provided were adopted by the board of directors of Windsor Hospice in 1987. None of these models, frameworks or statements can accommodate the practice of euthanasia and assisted suicide.

That is why we must address the following questions: "What type of theoretical, conceptual and ethical framework will now guide our teaching, policies, procedures and professional standards of practice? How will families be integrated into individualized care plans that include euthanasia and assisted suicide? What role will economics play in popularizing euthanasia as a means to rescue our cash-strapped healthcare system? Will economic considerations lead to a version of population control to cope with the anticipated "gray tsunami?"

Why patients either oppose or advocate euthanasia

A Swedish study conducted by Karlsson and colleagues reached the conclusion that

patients experiencing meaning and trust,
and who find strategies to handle suffering,
oppose euthanasia. In contrast, patients
with anticipatory fears of multidimensional
meaningless suffering, and with lack of belief
in the continuing availability of care, advocate
euthanasia. This indicates a need for healthcare
staff to address issues of trust, meaning, and
anticipatory fears.[18]

These goals can be achieved through the delivery of
sound hospice palliative care.

Echlin's own experience with individuals
suffering from advancing disease, leaves her with the
conviction that, provided they are assisted in developing
good coping strategies, people are able to redefine their
roles, and adapt to their changing cognitive (thinking)
function, their emotions, and their spirituality. In short,
they are enabled to redefine themselves in such a way
as to adapt to the new and often labile (unpredictable)
clinical course of their disease.

Dignity-conserving care

One of the most profound models of care was
conceived by Dr. Harvey Max Chochinov. In his paper
"Dignity conserving care-- a new model for Palliative
Care -- helping the patient feel valued," Chochinov
defines dignity as "the quality or state of being worthy,
honored, or esteemed." Tellingly, he observes that
"despite its unfortunate politicization by the assisted

---

18   M. Karlsson. "Suffering and Euthanasia: A qualitative study of
dying cancer patients' perspectives." Support Care Cancer 2012;20: pp.
1065-71.

suicide and euthanasia movements, dignity does not relate exclusively to considerations of assisted dying."[19] The model as it is published illustrates and includes the factors and sub-themes: dignity-related questions and therapeutic interventions that cover illness-related concerns, social dignity inventory and a dignity-conserving repertoire.

One example pertains to autonomy or control. The question asked of the patient is: "How in control do you feel?" and the therapeutic intervention is stated simply to "involve the patient in treatment and care decisions." When this dignity-conserving model is utilized in palliative care there is an emphasis on helping the patient understand that they are valued as a whole person. The model also includes an intriguing psychotherapy protocol. It is a helpful guide to clinicians in assessing the emotional and psychosocial wellbeing of their patients, and where their priorities lie. Chochinov demonstrates the power and value of this model when he declares, "it is no coincidence that patients who feel more appreciated are less likely to have considered euthanasia or physician-assisted suicide."[20]

The Respectful Death Model

Another excellent framework for care extending into end-of-life as well as providing concrete alternatives to euthanasia and assisted suicide, is the Respectful Death Model (RDM) described by Linda Wasserman. It addresses the need for a holistic approach and

19	H.M. Chochinov. "Dignity Conserving Care-A New Model for Palliative Care: Helping the Patient Feel Valued."JAMA 2002; 287(17): pp. 2253-60.
20	Chochinov. "Dignity Conserving Care", pp. 2253-60.

therapeutic relationship with patients and their families that ensure frank dialogue and respect.[21]

Spiritual or existential suffering

Addressing spiritual or existential suffering is another component of excellence in palliative hospice care that can be uncomfortable for doctors, nurses, social workers, and others on the inter-professional team to approach. This is due to the presence of diversity among individuals in a faith-based framework or the simple absence of a faith-based framework. Nonetheless, it is an essential facet of palliative care, since many individuals have a host of unresolved spiritual issues at the end of life. Take the following example.

Michael's story

Michael was a young man who shut himself off from his family and friends, and refused to share his life's journey with them. Michael opted to be alone in his suffering because he did not want to be a burden or cause further worry to his family and his friends. He avoided contact so that no one could witness his agony or embarrassment. Yet he honoured Echlin with a radical degree of openness. Michael was only sixteen. His diagnosis was Rhabdomyosarcoma (cancer involving muscle and bone) initially of the gluteal (hip) muscle. As the metastatic process of this disease progressed, his spinal cord became involved up to the level of the seventh thoracic vertebra (T7). Michael was also on the receiving end of offensive labels such as

---

21   L. Wasserman. *"Respectful Death: a model for end-of life care."* Clinical Journal of Oncology Nursing 2008; 12(4.): pp. 621-6.

"attention-seeking," "immature," "potential addict," "lazy teenager," "over-reactive," and "uncooperative." Why? Because there was no pathology visible at the time to explain his lack of mobility and extreme pain.

Michael's pain was horrific. It came in a lancinating (stabbing) manner -- he described it as an "electrical volt" descending from his lower spine, down into his right leg and throughout his pelvis. His pain was also visible. Large drops of perspiration stood out and ran off his forehead and upper lip. His pillows would get saturated as he rolled his head back and forth virtually writhing and crying out from the hurt and intensity of his pain. That kind of pain can only be known by the person experiencing it. Michael's singular plea was for help for his pain. When he became incontinent (loss of bowel and bladder control), he was sent for spinal decompression surgery. Following the disastrous findings during surgery he was totally paraplegic -- he lost the use of his lower limbs, bowel and bladder --and developed an infection. So very young, yet so burdened with pain, anxiety and aloneness.

At one point he let his defenses down and demanded, "What have I done that I should be punished like this? I have tried to be a good Christian. I've never used pot or booze. I don't fool around with girls like some of the guys do. I respect and honour my mom and dad. God must be very angry with me to make me suffer like this."

When Echlin asked if he felt abandoned, he answered "yes--even by God." Then he cried out in anguish.

Spiritual intervention: loving affirmation

Echlin and Michael talked about human love. The love that was offered to him as a person. It was necessary to acknowledge this daily, using the words "love" and "caring," affirming the life he lived and his very real concerns. They explored his profound fear of the unknown, despite his Christian faith in Jesus, as well as his belief in forgiveness and life eternal. They prayed together. As his disease progressed his doctors told him of its spread to his central nervous system (spinal column). He asked for detailed explanations, even requesting that diagrams be drawn of his spinal cord, the tumor growth, and how his spinal nerves were involved. The knowledge Echlin provided appeared to help him unexpectedly and to prepare him for what was coming. Michael's minister was tremendously supportive. He was kept apprised of Michael's physical and emotional status, his spiritual concerns, and his need for spiritual support and reassurance.

Managing "total pain"

Michael died in December 1981, just before his seventeenth birthday, having benefited from much spiritual care, and a deep sense of his own beliefs and inherent value as a person. He had received the spiritual care under the concept of "total pain." Unfortunately however, he did *not* have the benefit of a preventive and controlled pain regime. Nor did he experience any relief from an acute, unremitting anxiety that bordered many times on panic, and which could have been managed by carefully titrated anxiolytics (anti-anxiety medication). Here we have another horrendous story that teaches how implementing palliative care with specific focus on pain and symptom management as a first priority, would have made a critical difference. Michael and many others like him convict us of the overwhelming need to address human pain in all its dimensions beginning with the physical.

The horror of Michael's unnecessary suffering points to the need for all age levels (from the cradle to elderly) to be included in palliative care. In such cases we also need to master the understanding and knowledge of underlying pathophysiology (disease mechanisms and their effect on the person). The lack of pain management for Michael affected not only his life and death, but also his family and care providers who were tormented by feelings of anger and helplessness. Owing to the lack of narcotic and anxiolytic use, this type of intolerable and unbearable suffering still occurs today. That in turn is a significant factor in the insistent demand for assisted suicide and euthanasia.

Barriers to the proper treatment of pain

Currently there remain many barriers to effective assessment and treatment of physical pain. These include the mythology surrounding the use of opioids and addiction, a lack of knowledge on the part of the inter-professional team, barbaric attitudes towards pain, and a lack of adequate staffing patterns in both nursing and medicine.

The PCPCC publication *Not to Be Forgotten -- Care of Vulnerable Canadians* informs us that veterinarians receive five-times more education in pain control for animals than physicians do for human beings. In addition, 90 per cent of patients could obtain effective pain control, yet only 50 per cent do. Only 30 per cent of ordered pain medication is actually given, while 50 per cent of patients are left in moderate to severe pain after surgery, a situation which is not improving.[22] To us this is an indictment of medical and nursing professionals. In the words of Margaret Somerville,

> "people in pain have a right to fully adequate pain relief and treatment. Indeed for the health professional to act unreasonably in leaving a person in pain is a breach of a fundamental human right of the person. To unreasonably leave a person in pain is medical negligence (malpractice); and I believe in extreme cases, it should be treated as criminal negligence— wanton or reckless disregard for human life or safety. It is torture by willful omission.[23]

Good pain management will result in very few requests for physician-assisted suicide

If we promote hospice palliative care appropriately, and insist that our healthcare practitioners take pain and symptom management as seriously as the above statement says they should, there will be very few requests for euthanasia or physician-assisted suicide based on poorly-managed pain. In our opinion no person should have to die in intolerable pain. There may be rare cases where usual pain and symptom management

---

22   Albrecht et al. Parliamentary Committee on Palliative and Compassionate Care. *Not to Be Forgotten- Care of Vulnerable Canadians*, pp. 43-9. http://pcpcc-cpspsc.com/wp-content/uploads/2011/11/ReportEN.pdf
23   Quoted by Albrecht et al. *Not to be Forgotten*, pp. 43-4.

strategies fail in the final days of life, making palliative sedation a consideration. For example, in the last three to four days of life a small percentage of patients may develop a sudden escalation of symptoms such as pain, dyspnea (shortness of breath) or increasing anxiety, that are intolerable and refractory (not responsive) to routine therapies. At this point a medication that reduces consciousness may be used to sedate the patient into a rousable level where no pain will be felt. This palliative sedation is rarely necessary, but is effective in circumstances of such distress.[24]

Effective methods for physical pain and symptom management are the essential underpinning of excellent palliative care. We already possess the primary methods and tools for assessment, diagnosis, planning, intervention and evaluation on a whole-person basis. Details of pathophysiology, complete diagnostic information (X-rays, scans, lab values, etc.) and past medical history, including coping mechanisms, and current clinical status comprise the necessary data for a comprehensive assessment. Many pain assessment tools are already available: Visual Analogue Scales (VAS), Graphic Rating scales (GRS), simple description scales, facial expression rating scales, and Numeric Rating Scales (NRS). The palliative care team's assessment must indicate the type of pain, where it exists, pain intensity, as well as what alleviates and exacerbates the person's pain levels. The clinician must complete a concomitant assessment of the individual's emotional response to their pain, distressing symptoms and needs. As the

24   M.M. Dean et al. "Framework for Continuous Palliative Sedation Therapy in Canada." Journal of Palliative Medicine 2012; 15(8): pp. 870-9.

disease progresses, the symptom burden will change, and there must be constant re-assessment.

Some of the biggest challenges in these situations come from patients of other cultures or languages, persons with impaired speech and communication difficulties, and those who are unconscious. It must be stressed that lowered levels of consciousness do not mean an absence of pain. Anxiety must also be recognized and co-managed with physical pain. As Margo McCaffery, a nursing expert in pain management reminds us, "Before the introduction of the gate-control theory in 1965 by Melzack and Wall, very little appeared in the professional literature about pain. Pain control must be recognized as a priority."[25]

Psychosocial and spiritual pain

Once appropriate pain assessment and management has been carried out the psychosocial and spiritual domains must be assessed with sound interventions provided as needed. As we have emphasized, psychosocial and spiritual pain can only be managed after the patient's physical pain has been satisfactorily dealt with. We cannot expect any beneficial interventions to take effect as long as the patient is physically suffering.

Long-term palliative care

In 2013, Dr. Kathryn Pfaff, Sharon Thorpe and Jean Echlin (all on the nursing faculty at the University of Windsor) researched and presented a seminar-workshop sponsored by the deVeber Institute for

---

25   M. McCaffery and A. Beebe. *Pain: Clinical Manual for Nursing Practice*. Toronto: C.V. Mosby, 1989, p.1.

Bioethics and Social Research. The workshop was titled "Maximizing the Interprofessional Delivery of Palliative Care in Long-term Care."[26] The researchers highlighted the need for change and attention to pain management in long-term care facilities by presenting a case study involving Mrs. R.

Mrs. R.'s story of Alzheimer's-Type dementia

A 92-year-old resident in a long-term care facility, Mrs. R. was diagnosed with a late-stage Alzheimer's-Type Dementia. Her symptoms of agitation, irritability and aggression worsened with time, causing injury to herself, making care difficult for staff, and as well, causing further worry for her family. When Mrs. R. stopped eating and drinking, she was placed in what was called a "palliative bed" in a private room. The family and director of care consented to having an advanced practice nurse (APN) from outside the facility with clinical expertise in palliative care complete a comprehensive history and physical assessment. The Abbey Pain Scale[27] was used by the APN, who suspected moderate to severe pain particularly in Mrs. R's hips and spine. Based on her findings, the APN requested a pre-emptive lowest-dose trial of the opioid analgesic hydromorphone, 0.25mg every four hours around the clock. This was approved by the attending doctor and initiated by the nursing staff. The following day Mrs. R. resumed eating and drinking while also showing

---

26   Pfaff, K., Echlin, J., Thorpe, S., "The Problem of Pain in Persons with Dementia: The Challenges of Assessment and Management." Seminar workshop sponsored by The deVeber Institute for Bioethics and Social Research, 2013.

27   Dementia Care Australia Pty Ltd. *Abbey Pain Scale.* http://www. apsoc.org.au/PDF/Publications/4_Abbey_Pain_Scale.pdf

less agitation and aggression. After careful upwards titration of the Hydromorphone, Mrs. R was placed on a transdermal fentanyl (Duragesic) pain patch in which medication is absorbed through the skin, and began to walk and take day trips with her family. All this at the age of 92!

A comprehensive and systematic review of existing research showed barriers in the management of co-morbid pain among the elderly and persons with dementia.[28] These barriers included insufficient team communication and shared decision making, fundamental lack of resources, limited numbers of geriatricians, no nurse practitioners, replacement of Registered Nurses (RNs) with personal support workers (PSWs), lack of knowledge in assessment and management of pain,—even for those in long-term care who were able to communicate—archaic opinions about aging, pain and the use of opioids, and finally, outdated attitudinal problems among care providers.[29]

To this day, two years later, Mrs. R. remains mobile, is talking again in short sentences and is enjoying a better quality of life. Yet residents around her are suffering needlessly as evidenced by the sound of their crying out "help me—help me." Lack of visitors and busy staff mean these cries are ignored.

---

28   N. Menagh. "How collective wisdom improves quality of life in long-term care." Interdisciplinary Collaboration 2009; 20(1): pp.25-9; O. Ghandehari et al. "A controlled investigation of continuing pain education for long-term care staff." Pain Research Management 2013 18(1): pp.11-18.
29   Menagh. "How collective wisdom improves quality of life in long-term care," pp. 25-9; Ghandehari. "A controlled investigation of continuing pain education," pp. 11-18.

The need for a national Elder Abuse Strategy

In their first recommendation the PCPCC discuss the development of a National Elder Abuse Strategy.[30] They highlight cases of elder abuse including neglect. In light of current research on pain and the elderly, we are finding that far from being a rarity, elder abuse is a common problem. As we know from the experience of the Netherlands, the elderly are at continuing risk of euthanasia without consent.[31] In all likelihood many would never know that a lethal injection was going to be the means by which their life ended, nor would they know when it was coming.

Suicide Prevention vs Physician-Assisted Suicide

Since the Supreme Court has ruled that "intolerable and intractable emotional suffering" qualifies an individual for euthanasia or assisted suicide, it is ironic that Canada is at the same time hoping to implement a national Suicide Prevention Strategy. Introducing the Suicide Prevention section of the PCPCC document,[32] we need to look at the stigma and lack of quality care for our patients admitted to hospital in-patient psychiatric or mental-health units, particularly in smaller centers. A serious lack of physiotherapy, occupational-therapy or exercise programs and a total lack of any recreational schedule leave patients with no creative or physical

---

30   Albrecht, H., et al. *Not to Be Forgotten*, pp. 70-92.
31   A. van der Heide, B. Onwuteaka-Philipsen , M. Rurup, H. Buiting, J. van Delden, et al. "End of Life Practices in the Netherlands under the Euthanasia Act". *NEJM* 2007; 356: pp. 1957-65. See also Alex Schadenberg. *Exposing Vulnerable People to Euthanasia and Assisted Suicide*. London, ON: Ross Lattner, 2013, pp. 29-31.
32   Albrecht. et al. *Not to Be Forgotten*, pp. 70-92.

outlet except "shuffling" the halls while they are awake. This is conducive neither to healing nor to needed emotional expression. In some specialty psychiatric units there are no hospital beds, only mattresses on the floor. Patients who are acutely mentally ill are forced to sleep and eat on the floor. This appalling and uncivilized treatment is being inflicted in Canada in 2015 on the sickest persons with a diagnosis of mental illness. Under this particular setup patients requiring physical restraints are strapped to the floor on their mattress. Imagine how menacing staff must appear when being viewed from the floor. Such barbaric treatment of human beings results in more suffering, agitation, suicidal ideation and the increased use of major psychotropic drugs.

Because many staff (and patients) do not speak English as a first language, a barrier and additional stress are placed on verbal exchanges especially when the patient is in a panic or paranoid state. When staff members speak to one another in their native tongue, patients' anxiety and paranoia are increased, and they tend to interpret the conversation as mockery and ridicule against them. Another staffing problem affecting appropriate patient care is the standard practice of moving nursing staff to psychiatric units when they are no longer physically able to cope with the demands of medical or surgical nursing. The transfer to a psychiatric unit is an attempt to decrease their physical workload. But the consequence is that these members of nursing staff have no background or knowledge of psychiatric illness or mental health, nor any idea of patient rights under Ontario's Mental Health Act. More worrisome is the lack of knowledge of some staff about the use and side-effects of psychotropic drugs. Small wonder that many patients walk out the doors and head straight to suicide, or haunt the streets, feeling abandoned, emotionally weakened and devastated, and often homeless.

Even one change in psychiatric unit protocol would dramatically improve patient care in psychiatry and mental health. Routine or standing orders are a necessity, but they are sometimes missing. Standard/standing/routine orders are doctor-approved medications designed to be quickly available for crises in the event of a patient's sudden onset of pain, anxiety or panic. The medications under these orders are needed quickly when physicians are not on site or immediately available. Without these medications, endorsed in doctors' standing orders, a patient's condition can quickly deteriorate. As well, the medications are needed to prevent crises from escalating to the point where a patient will need physical restraints to prevent injury to themselves, to other patients and to staff. Symptoms in patients suffering mental illness can escalate quickly, inflicting more emotional damage on the individual suffering a "disease of the brain" if not appropriately and rapidly treated. Consider the following case study.

Mr. S.'s story of dementia

Mr. S. was admitted to acute care psychiatry/mental health with an initial diagnosis of dementia with increasingly aggressive behaviour and combativeness. He had many co-morbid medical-surgical conditions that had necessitated long-term use of opioids for pain and other medications for his deteriorating medical conditions. Although he was on morphine for pain management on admission, this was discontinued immediately. The consequence was that he suffered acute withdrawal symptoms in addition to his diagnosis of mental illness. This unfortunate gentleman also had kidney failure, inflammatory bowel disease, and congestive heart failure as a result of long-standing cardiovascular disease.

Because of activity limitations, bowel incontinence and a lack of access to sufficient home-healthcare, Mr. S. also had a large, painful decubitus (skin) ulcer extending across his coccyx, sacrum and buttocks. He asked simply for pain relief because "my pain is so cruel...I know I'm dying...and I'm ready." His primary nurse had enough conversations with Mr. S. to be certain that he was capable of making the decision to have his pain managed and other comfort measures. He tried in vain to refuse any more aggressive care and pushed staff away, who attempted to look after his physical needs, repeatedly asking to be left alone, often refusing to eat and drink, and crying out for help. He was denied pain control because the person with power of attorney (POA) vetoed it -- "at a physician's suggestion," she claimed -- and labelled him incompetent to make decisions about his need for pain management. As a consequence he had no relief for his physical pain and was given major psychotropic drugs that seemed to increase his depression, anxiety and realistic sadness.

Was assisted suicide the solution for Mr. S.?

Here we have yet another case in which euthanasia might well be the first solution to be considered when in reality all Mr. S. wanted was care and concern for his pain and other troublesome symptoms. He was clear that he merely wanted to be cared for, not killed. Yet if released from hospital in pain and without adequate symptom management, he might well have contemplated suicide. Failure to consider this man's request was torture for him, and showed a total disregard of his basic rights on the part of those providing his care.

Therefore we confront the paradox that a parliamentary committee is recommending a national suicide prevention program, at the very time that -- thanks to our Supreme Court -- we are pushing ahead full speed towards euthanasia and assisted suicide.

Is a compromise solution possible?

If we are not able to adopt palliative care as an inter-professional solution to this social disorder, a middle-ground or compromise must be found. One highly-touted solution would be the establishment of a new order of death managers that Chochinov calls "euthanologists."[33] If adopted, this would essentially remove the inflicting of death or facilitating suicide, out of the healthcare system. No doctor, nurse, long-term care institution or hospital would be obliged to

---

33   Harvey MaxChochinov. "Assisted Suicide Policy Needs to Account for the Human Ability to Overcome." Huffington Post May 26, 2015. http://www.huffingtonpost.ca/harvey-max-chochinov/access-to-palliative-care_b_7400566.html

participate against their religious, conscientious or professional judgment. If an order or association of euthanologists is established Chochinov raises the following questions:

- What professional designation will they require?

- What disciplines will they be drawn from?

- What training will they receive?

- What ethical and practice guidelines will they abide by?

- What judicial oversight will they submit to?[34]

In addition to the emergence of this new profession, the concept of death clinics and mobile units has been discussed for those wishing to die by assisted suicide at home in order to avoid institutional euthanasia. This is currently the model for euthanasia in the Netherlands.

The chief obstacle to the realization of this idea will doubtless come from "Dying with Dignity" groups and their supporters. Driven by emotionalism, fear mongering and euphemisms that cloud the issues, they have captured media attention without regard for the other side of the question. Yet we as a caring society ought to do everything humanly possible to prevent the stripping of the sick and disabled of their dignity. As we have shown, truly compassionate alternatives are currently available in the hospice palliative-care movement.

---

34   Chochinov, "Assisted Suicide Policy".

Conclusion

At the same time that the Supreme Court has struck down the Criminal Code provisions that protected vulnerable people from having their lives taken from them, an all-party committee of Parliament has been promoting alternatives to euthanasia and assisted suicide. The principles of palliative care, not just for the terminally ill, but for all those with serious chronic diseases, are well understood. We also know that when good palliative care is available the demand for assisted suicide almost evaporates. Yet over 70 per cent of Canadians do not have access to good palliative care. That is a major reason why the demand for unconditional personal autonomy has recently triumphed at the Supreme Court.

Legalized physician-assisted suicide will not only pose a danger to vulnerable people of all ages, it will compromise and corrupt the medical profession. It will turn some of them into killers. It will place an intolerable pressure on hospitals and long-term care institutions to betray their commitment to preserve but never to destroy human life. What is deeply disturbing is the intolerance behind the draft policy of the College of Physicians and Surgeons of Ontario (CPSO) towards doctors, nurses and institutions whose religious and ethical convictions and professional consciences do not permit them to make referrals for assisted suicide.

Many vulnerable people, most notably women, First Nations people and those with mental illness, will risk being steered toward a lethal injection. Not only that, opening wide the door to assisted suicide will make good palliative care difficult, as it has in the Netherlands. We have only just begun to free ourselves from the notion that palliative care is only for the dying. In fact it is for anyone with a serious life-threatening illness. But the Supreme Court ruling threatens to halt the progress made by the palliative-care profession over the past 40 years. Research in palliative care has introduced us to the treatment of "total pain", which includes not just physical, but psychological, social and spiritual pain. This is the direction in which we need to go.

Conclusion

As this book goes to press the **Quebec government** has announced that it will not wait for the federal government to craft a law establishing nationwide parameters for the practice of euthanasia and physician-assisted suicide. Jumping the gun, it will soon send all doctors in the province standardized kits with which to end the lives of any patients who wish that "service". All who are mentally fit, but suffering an incurable illness and in "constant and unbearable physical or psychological pain" will be eligible.[1] Although "unbearable psychological pain" usually means depression, there is no acknowledgement that depression is a treatable medical condition, still less any recognition that a person suffering depression is unfit to decide whether or not to end their life. Nonetheless, doctors are expected to cooperate, or if their conscience does not permit, to refer patients to a doctor whose conscience does. The health minister declared that "hospitals with palliative care units as well as palliative care homes must conform with the law and offer medical assistance to dying patients who ask for it".[2] In other words **hospitals and palliative-care hospices will not be allowed to honour their principles if they conflict with the new regime of euthanasia on demand.** This would appear to contradict the government's own legislation which calls upon palliative-care hospices to "adopt a code of ethics with respect to the rights of end-of-life patients

1   Sharon Kirkey, Quebec MDs to get euthanasia packages. National Post. Sept. 1, 2015, p. A1.

2   Quebec health minister insists physicians, institutions must help patients seeking medical aid in dying. Canadian Press. September 3, 2015.

and adopt a policy with respect to end-of life care."[3]

For all the assurances of strict safeguards to guarantee that new laws will not be abused, and that no one will be put to death without their knowledge and repeatedly-expressed consent, it has been clearly demonstrated that these safeguards are worthless in the Netherlands and Belgium. Many cases of euthanasia go unreported. The requirement that a second physician agree to the lethal injection is regularly ignored. People suffering from depression are put to death at their own request. Most disturbing of all, **large numbers of people in the Netherlands continue to be euthanized without their knowledge or consent, even when they are mentally competent to give that consent.**

Very recently we have been provided with a graphic illustration of the dishonesty that is likely to accompany the practice of euthanasia in Canada. In September 2015 it was revealed that Quebec's College of Physicians is poised to recommend that doctors should falsify death certificates by listing the underlying illness as the cause of death , rather than euthanasia. This stratagem is apparently designed to spare the feelings of the patient's family. Yet it will make it difficult if not impossible to track euthanasia numbers once the practice becomes legal. It will also involve doctors in dishonest activity. As lawyer Hugh Scher commented, "How is anybody supposed to have any confidence in a publicly administered system of euthanasia that is based upon a fraud?" **Falsifying**

---

3   *An Act Respecting End-of-Life Care*, RSQ c S-32.0001, s 1; http://www.assnat.qc.ca/en/travaux-parlementaires/projets-loi/projet-loi-52-40-1.html, Chap. III.16

death certificates will also render it difficult to know if the euthanasia was performed legitimately or not, whether consent was properly obtained, and if the legal safeguards were observed.[4]

In light of the difficulties encountered elsewhere it is strange that the Quebec government is rushing headlong into a regime of maximum availability of "assisted dying". Could it be that they hope it will reduce healthcare costs? Do they really believe that this is what people genuinely want? To be sure, public opinion polls show widespread support for euthanasia, but the same polls also show that few people want it for themselves. **Experience further shows that when people soberly weigh the pros and cons of legalization they become far less certain about its merits, and far more conscious of its perils.**[5]

The chief allure of legalized euthanasia and assisted suicide is that they empower people to decide for themselves when they will die. They promise that no one will be kept alive against their will, that they will not have to worry that when the time comes when they wish to die they will be physically unable to achieve their wish. In short these practices purport to enshrine personal autonomy.

This is the reasoning that has been recognized and upheld by the Supreme Court of Canada. But in enshrining personal autonomy the Court has turned its back on a centuries-old tradition that upheld the immeasurable value of human life, and made it a crime

---

4 Sharon Kirkey. Death be not honest. National Post Sept. 5, 2015, p. A4.

5 See above, Introduction, p. 1.

to help anyone to kill themselves. It has also chosen to ignore the prudential reasons behind the Criminal Code prohibition on "assisted dying". These reasons have to do with public safety, the principle that suicide and killing are not reasonable or controllable problem-solving strategies, and the principle that older or mentally-ill people should not be steered toward hastened death. **Once the practice of "assisted dying" becomes legal people who are not even dying will become targets.** There will be less incentive to pursue the improvement of palliative care for the seriously, chronically or terminally ill. There will be an ever rising temptation for cash-strapped hospitals, relatives and caregivers with an agenda to cut short expenses and hasten the arrival of an inheritance by promoting "assisted dying".

Once euthanasia and assisted suicide become normal practice the number of cases will inexorably increase from year to year, as the experience of Holland, Belgium, Oregon and Washington has proven. As the numbers grow, so will the tendency to turn the use of the legal "guidelines" into an empty ritual.

Thus, a large number of cases regularly go unreported in Europe – close to one-half in Belgium. Although the numbers have shrunk from previous highs, as many as 200 people per year are still put to death in the Netherlands without their knowledge or consent, *even though they were competent to give that consent.* In jurisdictions where it is legal, euthanasia can only be performed by a physician. Yet nurses are administering lethal injections, and some nurses are taking matters into their own hands, administering them without a physican's authorization. It is a normal requirement that a second physician be consulted, yet this requirement is also widely flouted. Despite the widespread breaches of the law that have been brought to light in published studies, no charges have ever been laid against a physician in Belgium for such breaches. In the Netherlands a handful of cases have been brought to trial, but there have been no convictions. **Legal safeguards have therefore proved to be a weak reed when it comes to protecting the vulnerable from being killed without their consent.**

There are other causes for disquiet. In countries where it has been practised for a long time, the net has been cast steadily wider and wider to include those who it was never imagined would be eligible for "assisted dying". **Infants perfectly capable of surviving with normal care are now being euthanized in the Netherlands.** In the same country adolescent children, with their well-known vulnerability to suicidal thoughts, can also apply for euthanasia between the ages of twelve and seventeen with their parents' consent. Depression is a treatable psychological condition that comes and goes even when it is untreated. A depressed person is in no condition to make decisions about their own life and death. Yet more and more cases are coming to light of **people whose only medical condition is depression being granted euthanasia** on the grounds of "intolerable suffering". When such people are euthanized they **often leave behind a legacy of sorrow and anguish to their families** or loved ones, especially when those close to them have only been informed of the suicide after the fact.

At the same time a wide-open regime of "assisted dying" contains many seeds of corruption. Family members impatient for an inheritance will find it easier to pressure an elderly relative to agree to "assisted dying". Governments will be increasingly tempted to abandon good palliative care in favour of the cheaper option of euthanasia on demand. This is exactly what has happened in the Netherlands. Those doctors who participate in the administration of euthanasia will be corrupted too, as they abandon their age-old commitment to heal and preserve life in favour of destroying it.

Are there any alternatives to Quebec's enthusiastic embrace of assisted dying? There is no need to regard Quebec as being on the cusp of human progress. It is worth recalling that the vast majority of the world rejects euthanasia and assisted suicide. Instead of following Quebec's example, we may hope that the Federal Government's Expert Panel will insist on strict harm-reduction measures to ensure that "assisted dying" is offered only in the context where death is truly imminent. **Let us hope too that the new law is hedged in with the most stringent safeguards to protect all of us.** The choices created by an assisted-death law may belong not to us but to others around us, who can have their own agenda. If it is unavoidable to create such a law, there ought to be a new order of "death managers" or "euthanologists", leaving undamaged the vocation of doctors, nurses and medical institutions to preserve rather than destroy life. Everyone who desires "assisted dying" should have their application approved by an independent third party, preferably a judge.

But there is another approach that Parliament ought to consider. In September 2015 the Association for Reformed Political Action (ARPA) of Canada issued a report supporting passage of a law clarifying for the Supreme Court the true purpose of a total ban on assisted suicide. It would be "to protect every human life, to maintain respect for the sanctity and inviolability of life, to affirm the equal worth of every life, and to prohibit as a public wrong the participation of any person in the deliberate, active participation in another person's suicide with or without the latter person's consent."[6] In other words, Parliament has the authority, which it ought to exercise, to correct the Supreme Court's mistaken interpretation of the Criminal Code's ban on assisted suicide in sections 14 and 241(b) as being intended solely to protect vulnerable people from being killed without their consent.

More positively, and regardless of what law Parliament ultimately passes, steps are urgently required to provide everyone who needs it with high quality pain control and palliative care. Canada, as one of the most affluent countries in the world, can surely afford to do this for its elderly population. After all, it has been shown again and again that **when people's pain is properly managed in the context of high-quality, compassionate palliative care, there is very little demand, and no need, for assisted suicide or euthanasia.**

---

6   "John Sikkema. *Protecting Life: How Parliament Can Fully Ban Assisted Suicide without Section 33*. Ottawa: ARPA Canada, 2015, p. 5.

References

Abbreviations

BMJ British Medical Journal

BMC BioMedCentral Medicine

CMAJ Canadian Medical Association Journal
JAMA Journal of the American Medical Association
NEJM New England Journal of Medicine

PRIMARY:

AC v Manitoba (Director of Child and Family Services), 2009 SCC 30, [2009] 2 SCR 181

Assisted suicide: strengthening the right of self-determination. Swiss Federal Department of Justice and Police. Retrieved from http://www.ejpd.admin.ch/ejpd/en/home/aktuell/news/2011/2011-06-29.html

Blencoe v British Columbia (Human Rights Commission), 2000 SCC 44, [2000] 2 SCR 307

Canada (Attorney General) v Bedford, 2013 SCC 72, [2013] 3 SCR 1101

Canadian Charter of Rights and Freedoms, Part I of the Constitution Act, 1982, being Schedule B to the Canada Act 1982 (UK), 1982, c 11, s 7.

Carter v Canada, 2012 BCSC 886, 287 CCC (3d) 1

Carter v Canada, 2013 BCCA 435, 51 BCLR (5th) 213

Carter v Canada, 2015 SCC 15, [2015] 1 SCR 331

Code of Ethics of Quebec Physicians, c M-9, r 17, s 58; http://www2.publicationsduquebec.gouv.qc.ca/dynamicSearch/telecharge.php?type=3&file=/M_9/M9R17_A.HTM

Criminal Code of Canada, RSC 1985, c C-46.

Criminal Code of Canada, RSC 1985, c C-46. http://laws-lois.justice.gc.ca/eng/acts/C-46/

Death with Dignity Act. Washington State Department of Health. Retrieved from http://www.doh.wa.gov/YouandYourFamily/IllnessandDisease/DeathwithDignityAct

End-of-life Debate. (2015, March 10). Retrieved July 11, 2015 from http://www.gouvernement.fr/en/end-of-life-debate

Euthanasia, assisted suicide and non-resuscitation on request. The Government of the Netherlands. Retrieved from http://www.government.nl/issues/euthanasia/euthanasia-assisted-suicide-and-non-resuscitation-on-request

Fleming v Reid, 4 OR (3d) 74 (CA)

German Criminal Code, Section 216, translated by Michael Bohlander (2015)

History of Euthanasia in the UK - Lipscombe S., Barber S.. Assisted Suicide. Library House of Commons. (2014, Aug 20).

Lords Hansard. 7 July 2009 : Column 614 . Retrieved from http://www.publications.parliament.uk/pa/ld200809/ldhansrd/text/90707-0008.htm#09070778000031

Medische Beslissingen Rond Het Levenseinde. I: Rapport van de Commissie Onderzoek Medische Praktijk ionzake Euthanasie. II: Het Onderzoek voor de Commissie Medische Praktijk inzake Euthanasie (Medical Decisions about the End of Life: I: Report of the Committee to Study the Medical Practice Concerning Euthanasia. II: The Study for the Committee of Medical Practice Concerning Euthanasia) also known as Remmelink Report. The Hague: SDU Publishers, Plantijnstraat, 2 vols., 1991.

National Assembly [Quebec]. Bill 52: An Act Respecting End-of-Life Care (2014), http://www.dyingwithdignity.ca/database/files/library/final_of_quebec_bill.pdf

National Assembly [Quebec]. Select Committee: Dying With Dignity Report (March 2012); http://www.dyingwithdignity.ca/database/files/library/Quebec_death_with_dignity_report.pdf

Oregon Public Health Division. About the Death With Dignity Act. Oregon Health Authority. Retrieved from https://public.health.oregon.gov/ProviderPartnerResources/EvaluationResearch/DeathwithDignityAct/Pages/faqs.aspx

Oregon Public Health Division. Oregon's Death with Dignity Act Report, 2014. https://public.health.oregon.gov/ProviderPartnerResources/EvaluationResearch/DeathwithDignityAct/Documents/year17.pdf

Original legislation permitting euthanasia in 1995: http://www.nt.gov.au/lant/parliamentary-business/committees/rotti/rotti95.pdf

Parliament of Canada. "Library of Parliament Research Publications: Euthanasia and Assisted Suicide in Canada" (February 2013); http://www.parl.gc.ca/Content/LOP/ResearchPublications/2010-68-e.htm#a11

Parliament of Canada. "Private Member's Bill, 40th Parliament, 3rd Session, C-384" http://www.parl.gc.ca/LegisInfo/BillDetails.aspx?Language=E&Mode=1&billId=4328668

Parliament of Canada. "Private Member's Bill, 41st Parliament, 2nd Session, C-581" http://www.parl.gc.ca/LEGISInfo/BillDetails.aspx?Language=E&Mode=1&billId=6477659

Parliament of Canada. "Private Member's Bill, 41st Parliament, 2nd Session, C-582" http://www.parl.gc.ca/LEGISInfo/BillDetails.aspx?Language=E&Mode=1&billId=6477700

Patient Choice and Control at End of Life Act (Act 39). Vermont Department of Health Agency of Human Services. Retrieved from http://healthvermont.gov/family/end_of_life_care/patient_choice.aspx#law

R v Latimer, [1997] 1 SCR 217, 2001 SCC 1

Republic of Colombia Constitutional Court, Sentence # c-239/97, Ref. Expedient # D-1490, May 20, 1997.)

Remmelink Report. *See* Medische Beslissingen Rond Het Levenseinde

Rodriguez v British Columbia, [1993] 3 SCR 519, 107 DLR (4th) 342 (SCC)

Royal Dutch Medical Association (KNMG). "Guideline for Palliative Sedation". Utecht, The Netherlands: January 2009, p. 6. http://knmg.artsennet.nl/Publicaties/KNMGpublicatie/66978/Guideline-for-palliative-sedation-2009.htm

Scott v Cousins (2001), 37 ETR (2d) 113 (Ont SCJ).

Swiss Criminal Code of 21 December 1937, https://www.admin.ch/opc/en/classified-compilation/19370083/index.html#a115

The Special Senate Committee on Euthanasia and Assisted Suicide. Of Life and Death - Final Report (June 1995); http://www.parl.gc.ca/Content/SEN/Committee/351/euth/rep/lad-tc-e.htm

Termination of Life on Request and Assisted Suicide (Review Procedures) Act 2002 [Netherlands]. Retrieved from http://www.eutanasia.ws/documentos/Leyes/Internacional/Holanda%20Ley%202002.pdf

The Washington Death With Dignity Act. Washington State Legislature. Chapter 70.245 RCW. Retrieved from http://app.leg.wa.gov/rcw/default.aspx?cite=70.245&full=true

Washington State Department of Health, Death With Dignity Act. http://www.doh.wa.gov/YouandYourFamily/IllnessandDisease/DeathwithDignityAct

SECONDARY:

Scientific Papers and Official Publications

Albrecht Harold, Joseph Comartin, Frank Valeriote, Kelly Block, Francis Scarpaleggia. *Not to be Forgotten: Care of Vulnerable Canadians.* Ottawa: Parliamentary Committee on Palliative and Compassionate Care, 2011.

An open letter to all Members of Parliament and of the House of Lords, from leaders of British faith communities of Buddhists, Christians, Hindus, Jews, Muslims and Sikhs, expressing grave concern at continuing and renewed efforts to legalise euthanasia – 2005.

Bakitas, Marie, Lyons Kathleen, Hegel Mark, Balan Stefan, Brokaw Frances, Seville Janette, Hull Jay, Li Zhongze, Tosteson Tor, Byock Ira, and Ahles, Tim. "The Project ENABLE II Randomized Controlled Trial to Improve Palliative Care for Patients with Advanced Cancer". JAMA Vol. 302, No. 7 (August 2009): 741-749.

Barf HA, Post MWM, Verhoef M, Jennekens-Schinkel A, Gooskens RH, and Prevo AJ. "Life satisfaction of young adults with spina bifida." Developmental Medicine and Child Neurology 49; (2007): 458-463.

Barry S. "Quality of Life and Myelomeningocele: An Ethical and Evidence Based Analysis of the Groningen Protocol." Pediatric Neurosurgery 46:409-414 (2010).

Baumann, A., Audibert, G., Claudot, F., & Puybasset, L. (2009). Ethics review: End of life legislation the French model. Critical Care, 13(1), 204. doi:10.1186/cc7148.

Bilsen J, Chambaere K, Cohen J, Deliens L, Mortier F, and Pousset G. "Medical End-of-Life Decisions in Children in Flanders, Belgium A Population-Based Postmortem Survey." Archives of Pediatric Adolescent Medicine 164(6); (2010): 547-553.

Bilsen J, Chambaere K, Cohen J, Deliens L, Onwuteaka-Philipsen B, and Mortier F. "Physician assisted deaths under the euthanasia law in Belgium: a population-based survey." CMAJ 182(9): 895-901 (June 15, 2010).

Bilsen J, Cohen J, Deliens L, Mortier F, Rurup M, and Smets T. "Reporting of euthanasia in medical practice in Flanders Belgium: cross sectional analysis of reported and unreported cases." BMJ 341:c5174 (2010).

Bilsen J, Deliens L, Inghelbrecht E, and Mortier F. "The role of nurses in physician-assisted deaths in Belgium." CMAJ 182 (9) (June 15, 2010).

Blacksher, E. Euthanasia in Australia. The Hastings Center Report, 25(5), 47 (1995). Retrieved from http://search.proquest.com/docview/222378814?accountid=14771

Bowman RM, McLone DG, Grant JA, Tomita T, and Ito JA. "Spina bifida outcome: a 25-year prospective." Pediatric Neurosurgy 34: 114–120 (2001).

Bregie D. Onwuteaka-Philipsen et al. "Euthanasia and other end-of-life decisions in the Netherlands in 1990, 1995, and 2001". The Lancet. 2 Aug. 2003; 362 (9381): pp. 395-9.http://image.thelancet.com/extras/03art3297web.pdf

Breitbart W, Rosenfeld B, Pessin H, et al. "Depression, Hopelessness, and Desire for Hastened Death in Terminally Ill Patients With Cancer," JAMA; 284(22) (2000):2907-2911. http://jama.jamanetwork.com/article.aspx?articleid=193350

Butts C, "Belgium's 'sad path' for assisted suicide" One News Network, July 2015, http://www.onenewsnow.com/pro-life/2015/07/22/belgiums-sad-path-for-assisted-suicide

Caires l, Juliana S., de Andradel TA, do Amaral J, de Andrade Calasans MT, and da Silva Rocha, MD. "The Use of Complementary Theories in Palliative Care: Benefits and Purposes". Cogitare Enfermagem (July/September 2014): 471-477.

Canadian Hospice Palliative Care Association. "Palliative Care in the Community: An Environmental Scan of Frameworks and Indicators, the Way Forward Initiative: An Integrated Palliative Approach to Care". (June 2013): 1-55.

Canadian Hospice Palliative Association. Mission and Vision. http://www.chpca.net/about-us/mission-and-vision.aspx

Canadian Medical Association, Euthanasia and Assisted Death *(Update 2014)*, p. 3. http://www.cma.ca/Assets/assets-library/ document/en/advocacy/EOL/CMA_Policy_Euthanasia_ Assisted%20Death_PD15-02-e.pdf

Canadian Nurses Association. *Code of Ethics.* (June 2008). http://cna-aiic.ca/~/media/cna/page-content/pdf-en/code_of_ ethics_2008_e.pdf

Canadian Society of Palliative Care Physicians. *Position Statement Following Supreme Court Judgment re: Carter* (February 12, 2015) http://www.cspcp.ca/wp-content/uploads/2014/10/CSPCP-Position-Following-SCC-Judgment-12-Feb-2015.pdf

Chambaere K, Bilsen J, Cohen J, Onwuteaka-Philipsen BD, Mortier F, Deliens L. "Trends in medical end-of-life decision making in Flanders, Belgium 1998-2001-2007." Med Decis Making; 31 (3) (May-June 2011): 500-510.

Chambaere K, Cohen J, Mortier F, and Vander Stichele R. "Recent Trends in Euthanasia and Other End of Life Practices in Belgium." NEJM; 372; 12. (March 19 2015). http://www.nejm.org/ doi/pdf/10.1056/NEJMc1414527.

Chochinov HM, Clinch JJ, Enns M, Lander S, Levitt M, Mowchun N, and Wilson KG. "Desire for Death in the Terminally Ill." American Journal of Psychiatry 152; 8:1185-91 (August, 1995).

Chochinov Harvey M. "Assisted Suicide Policy Needs to Account for the Human Ability to Overcome." Huffington Post May 26, 2015. http://www.huffingtonpost.ca/harvey-max-chochinov/access-to-palliative-care_b_7400566.html

Chochinov, Harvey M. "Dignity-Conserving Care—A New Model for Palliative Care: Helping the Patient Feel Valued". JAMA 287 (17); (May 2002): 2253-2260.

Chochinov, Harvey M. "We have a right to die but not to quality palliative care." *The Province*. Feb. 24, 2015. http:\ \www.the province.com/story print.html?id=10837975&sponsor=true

Christian Medical Dental Society - Canada. http://www. cmdscanada.org/ConscienceProtection.aspx

Clin, B., & Ferrant, O. Law of 22 April 2005 on patients' rights and the end of life in France: Setting the boundaries of euthanasia, with regard to current legislation in other European countries. Medicine, Science and the Law, (2010): 183-188.

Collège des médecins du Québec. "Physicians, Appropriate Care and the Debate on Euthanasia – A Reflection" (October 2009); http://www.cmq. org/en/Medias/Profil/Commun/Nouvelles/2009/~/ media/208E2B537FB144FAAE33DEB458D3AA90.ashx?91027

College of Physicians and Surgeons of Ontario. Professional Obligations and Human Rights. http://policyconsult.cpso.on.ca/ wp-content/uploads/2014/12/Draft-Professional-Obligations-and-Human-Rights.pdf

Dean M et al. "Framework for Continuous Palliative Sedation Therapy in Canada." Journal of Palliative Medicine 2012; 15(8): pp. 870-879.

Delight E, and Goodall J. "Babies with spina bifida treated without surgery: parents' views on home versus hospital care." BMJ 297; (1988): 1230–1233.

Dementia Care Australia Pty Ltd. Abbey Pain Scale. http://www. apsoc.org.au/PDF/Publications/4_Abbey_Pain_Scale.pdf

Dempsey, Laura, Dowling Maura, Larkin Philip, and Murphy, Kathy. "The Unmet Palliative Care Needs of Those Dying with Dementia". International Journal of Palliative Nursing. 21 (3); (March 2015): 126-133.

De zaak-Prins, Hof Amsterdam November 7 1995, TvGR 1996, pp. 30-6 [The Prins case].

Donker G, Slotman F, and A Francke. Palliative sedation in Dutch general practice from 2005-2011. *British Journal of General Practice* October 2013, p. 669.

Echlin Jean. "Supreme Court Assisted Dying Disorder: A New Social Disorder." Euthanasia Prevention Coalition Newsletter. 162; (May 2015): 3.

Emanuel E, Fairclough D, Emanuel L. "Attitudes and Desires Related to Euthanasia and Physician-Assisted Suicide Among Terminally Ill Patients and Their Caregivers." JAMA 284 (19); (2000): 2460-2468. http://jama.jamanetwork.com/article. aspx?articleid=193281

Emanuel EJ. "The Practice of euthanasia and physician-assisted suicide in the United States: adherence to proposed safeguards and effects on physicians." JAMA 280 (6); (1998): 507-13.

"Ethics Council rejects assisted suicide law". The Local. (2014, December 19). Retrieved June 22 2015.

"Euthanasia and assisted suicide laws around the world". The Guardian (2014, July 17) Accessed June 9, 2015 from http:// www.theguardian.com/society/2014/jul/17/euthanasia-assisted-suicide-laws-world

"Explanation of the Dutch Law". World Federation of Right to Die Societies. Retrieved July 5, 2015 from http://www.worldrtd. net/qanda/physician-assisted-suicide-same-euthanasia

"French parliament votes through 'deep sleep' law for terminally ill". Guardian (2015, March 17). http://www.theguardian. com/world/2015/mar/17/french-parliament-deep-sleep-law-terminally-ill-euthanasia

Ganzini L, Goy ER and Dobscha SK. "Why Oregon patients request assisted death: family members' views." J Gen Intern Med. 23(2); (2008): 154–57. http://www.ncbi.nlm.nih.gov/pmc/articles/PMC2265314/

Ganzini L, Johnston W, McFarland B, Tolle S, Lee M. "Attitudes of Patients with Amyotrophic Lateral Sclerosis and Their Care Givers toward Assisted Suicide," NEJM 339 (1998): 967-73. http://www.nejm.org/doi/full/10.1056/NEJM199810013391406#t=articleResults

"German Medical Association: Principles regarding the accompaniment of the dying process by physicians". German Reference Centre for Ethics in the Life Sciences (DRZE). Retrieved June 17, 2015 http://www.drze.de/in-focus/euthanasia/legal-regulations

Ghandehari O, et al. "A controlled investigation of continuing pain education for long-term care staff." Pain Research Management 2013 18(1): pp.11-18.

Greer, Joseph, Pirl William, Jackson Vicki, Muzikansky Alona, Lennes Inga, Heist Rebecca, Gallagher Emily, and Temel, Jennifer. "Effect of Early Palliative Care on Chemotherapy Use and End-of-Life Care in Patients With Metastatic Non–Small-Cell Lung Cancer". Journal of Clinical Oncology 30 (4); (February 2012): 394-396.

Guthier S, Mausbach J, Reisch T, and Bartsch C. "Suicide tourism: a pilot study on the Swiss phenomenon." Journal of Medical Ethics. (August 20, 2015); 41(8):611-617. 10.1136/medethics-2014-102091.

Horne-Thompson Anne and Bramley Rebecca. "The Benefits of Interdisciplinary Practice in a Palliative Care Setting: a Music Therapy and Physiotherapy Pilot Project". Progress in Palliative Care 19 (6); (2011): 304-08.

Hughes Ridian. "National Dementia Strategy". British Journal of Healthcare Assistants 3 (7); (July 2009): 348-349.

Hunt GM, and Oakeshott P. "Outcome in people with open spina bifida at age 35: prospective community based cohort study." BMJ 326; (2003):1365–6.

Hurst SA and Mauron A. "Assisted suicide and euthanasia in Switzerland: allowing a role for non-physicians." BMJ, 326(7383) (2003), 271–273.

Jansen-van der Weide Marijke, Onwuteaka-Philipsen Bregje D, van der Wal Gerrit. "Requests for Euthanasia and Physician-assisted Suicide and the Availability and Application of Palliative Options". Palliative and Supportive Care 4; (2006): 399–406.

Jong TH. "Deliberate termination of life of newborns with spina bifida, a critical reappraisal." Childs Nerv Syst 24; (2008):13-28.

Karlsson M, Milberg A, Strang P. "Suffering and euthanasia: a qualitative study of dying cancer patients' perspectives." Support Care Cancer 20 (5); (May 2011):1065-71.

Kompanje EJO, T.H.R. de Jong, W.F.M. Arts, J.J. Roteveel. "Problematische basis voor 'uitzichtloos en ondraaglijk lijden' als criterium voor actieve levensbeëindiging bij pasgeborenen met spina bifida". [Problematical basis for 'hopeless and unbearable suffering' as a criterion for active euthanasia in newborns with spina bifida] Ned Tijdschr Geneeskd 2005 10 September;r49:2067-9.

Koninklijke Nederlandsche Maatschapptij tot bevordering der Geneeskunst (KNMG -- Royal Dutch Medical Association). The role of the physician in the voluntary termination of life. June 2011, p. 23.

Lohman, Diederik, Schleifer Rebecca, and Amon, Joseph. "Access to Pain Treatment as a Human Right." BMC Medicine 8 (8); (20 January 2010).

Manninen BA. "A case for justified non-voluntary active euthanasia: exploring the ethics of the Groningen Protocol."*J Med Ethics* 32 (11); Nov. 2006: 643-51, p. 650.

Marijke C et al. "Requests for euthanasia and physician assisted suicide, and the availability and application of palliative options". Palliative and Supportive Care 4; (2006): 399-406.

Matthews, Hugh. "Better Palliative Care Could Cut Euthanasia". BMJ 317; (12 December 1998): 1613.

McAlpine, CH. "Elder abuse and neglect". Age Ageing 37; (2008): 151-160.

McPherson, Christine J., Keith G. Wilson, and Mary Ann Murray. 2007. "Feeling like a Burden to Others: A Systematic Review Focusing on the End of Life." *Palliative Medicine* 21: 115-128.

Ménard, Jean-Pierre et al., Mettre en œuvre les recommandations de la Commission spéciale de l'Assemblée nationale sur la question de mourir dans la dignité: Rapport du Comité de juristes experts (January 2013); http://www.dyingwithdignity.ca/database/files/library/rapport_comite_juristes_experts.pdf

Menagh N. "How collective wisdom improves quality of life in long-term care." Interdisciplinary Collaboration 2009; 20(1): pp.25-29.

Mock, Vanessa. "Luxembourg monarch muzzled over euthanasia," The Independent [London], 11 December 2008. http://www.parl.gc.ca/content/lop/researchpublications/2011-67-e.htm#ftn83

Montana Death with Dignity Act. Patients Rights Council. Retrieved from http://www.patientsrightscouncil.org/site/montana/ - Official Bill for Montana Death With Dignity Act 2008 - http://leg.mt.gov/bills/2015/BillPdf/SB0202.pdf

Narayanasamy, Aru. "Palliative Care and Spirituality". Indian J Palliative Care 13 (2); (December 2007): 32-41.

"Netherlands, first country to legalize euthanasia". Bulletin of the World Health Organization, 2001, p.79. Retrieved from http://www.ncbi.nlm.nih.gov/pmc/articles/PMC2566446/pdf/11436481.pdf

Nicol J, Tiedemann M, Valiquet D. "Euthanasia and Assisted Suicide: International Experiences". Library of Parliament Research Publications (25 Oct. 2013). http://www.parl.gc.ca/content/lop/researchpublications/2011-67-e.htm#ftn83

Noble Agnes and Jones Colin. "Benefits of Narrative Therapy: Holistic Interventions at the End of Life". British Journal of Nursing 14 (6); (2005): 330-333.

Onwuteaka-Philipsen BD et al. *Evaluatie wet toetsing levensbeëindiging op verzoek en hulp bij zelfdoding* [*Evaluation of the Dutch Euthanasia Act of 2002*]. Den Haag: ZonMw, 2007, p. 112.

Onwuteaka-Philipsen, BD et al. "Euthanasia and other end-of-life decisions in the Netherlands in 1990, 1995, and 2001". The Lancet 2 Aug. 2003; 362 (9381): 395-399.

Oregon Health Authority. "Oregon Older Adult Suicide Prevention Plan: A Call to Action". (March 2006).

"Oregon's Death with Dignity Act: The First Year's Experience," Oregon Health Division Report, (Feb 18, 1999).

Oregon Public Health Division. "Oregon's Death with Dignity Act." (2014) http://public.health.oregon.gov/ProviderPartnerREsources/EvaluationResearch/DeathwithDignityAct/Documents/year17.pdf

Pereira, Jose. "Legalizing euthanasia or assisted suicide: the illusion of safeguards and controls." Current Oncology 18:2 (2011): e38–e45.

Robert Baxter vs. Supreme Court of Montana. Montana Supreme Court, decided 2009. http://www.patientsrightscouncil.org/site/wp-content/uploads/2011/03/Montana_Opinion_12_31_09.pdf

Senate of Canada, Quality End-of-Life Care: The Right of Every Canadian. Report of the Subcommittee to Update of Life and Death (June 2000).

Senate of Canada. Of Life and Death, Report of the Special Senate Committee on Euthanasia and Assisted Suicide (June 1995).

Seymour, Jane, Bellamy Gary, Gott Merryn, Ahmedzai Sam H., and Clark David. "Good Deaths, Bad Deaths: Older People's Assessments of the Risks and Benefits of Morphine and Terminal Sedation in End-of Life Care". Health, Risk & Society 4 (3); (2002): 288-301.

Silvoniemi M, Vasankari T, Vahlberg T, Clemens K and Salminen E. "Physicians' attitudes towards euthanasia in Finland: would training in palliative care make a difference?" Palliative Medicine 24 (7); (October 2010):744-746.

"The Situation in the Federal Republic of Germany". German Reference Centre for Ethics in the Life Sciences (DRZE): Retrieved June 17 2015 http://www.drze.de/in-focus/euthanasia/legal-regulations

Smets T, Bilsen J, Cohen J, Rurup M, Keyser E, and Deliens L. "The Medical Practice of Euthanasia in Belgium and the Netherlands: Legal notification, control, and evaluation process." Elsvier Health Policy 90; (2009): 181-187.

Smets T, Bilsen J, Cohen J, Mette L, Rurup L, and Deliens L . "Legal Euthanasia in Belgium: Characteristics of All Reported Euthanasia Cases". Medical Care 2009; 47(12), p. 1. http://www.worldrtd.net/sites/default/files/u22/Smets_reported%20euthanasia%20cases_Med%20Care.pdf. Accessed July 23, 2015.

Somerville Margaret. "Euthanasia and Assisted Suicide: A Physician's and Ethicist's Perspectives." Medicolegal and Bioethics 4; (2014): 1-12.

Temel Jennifer, Greer Joseph, Muzikansky Alona, Gallagher Emily, Admane Sonal, Jackson Vicki, Dahlin Constance, Blinderman Craig, Jacobsen Juliet, Pirl William, Billings Andrew, and Lynch, Thomas. "Early Palliative Care for Patients with Metastatic Non–Small-Cell Lung Cancer". NEJM 363 (8); (August 2010): 733-742.

Thienpont Lieve, Verhofstadt Monica, Van Loon Tony, Distelmans Wim, Audenaert Kurt, De Deyn Peter P. "Euthanasia requests, procedures and outcomes for 100 Belgian patients suffering from psychiatric disorders: a retrospective, descriptive study." BMJ Open 2015 Jul 27;5(7):: 5:e007454.

Udo Schuklenk et al. End-of-Life Decision Making. The Royal Society of Canada (November 2011); http://rsc-src.ca/sites/default/files/pdf/RSCEndofLifeReport2011_EN_Formatted_FINAL.pdf

van de Scheur Ada and van der Arend Arie. "The Role of Nurses in Euthanasia: A Dutch Study". Nursing Ethics 5(6); (November 1998): 497-508

Van der Heide A, Onwuteaka-Philipsen B, Rurup M, Buiting H, van Delden J, et al. "End of Life Practices in the Netherlands under the Euthanasia Act." NEJM 356; (2007): 1957-1965.

van Soest-Poortvlietl Mirjam, van der Steenl JT, de Vet HCW, Hertoghl CMPM, Deliens Luc, and Onwuteaka-Philipsen BD. "Comfort Goal of Care and End-of-Life Outcomes in Dementia: A Prospective Study". *Palliative Medicine* 29 (6); (2015): 538-546

Verhagen E. "The Groningen Protocol- Euthanasia in Severely Ill Newborns". NEJM 352 (10); (March 10, 2005) p 960-962.

Washington State Department of Health, 2009 Death With Dignity Act Report. http://www.doh.wa.gov/portals/1/Documents/5300/DWDA2009.pdf

Washington State Department of Health, 2013 Death With Dignity Act Report. http://www.doh.wa.gov/portals/1/Documents/Pubs/422-109-DeathWithDignityAct2013.pdf

Washington State Department of Health. 2012 Death With Dignity Act Report. http://www.doh.wa.gov/portals/1/Documents/Pubs/422-109-DeathWithDignityAct2012.pdf

Washington State Department of Health. "Washington State Department of Health 2013 Death With Dignity Act Report. Executive Summary."

Washington State Department of Health. "Washington State Department of Health 2014 Death With Dignity Act Report. Executive Summary." http://www.doh.wa.gov/portals/1/Documents/Pubs/422-109-DeathWithDignityAct2014.pdf

Wasserman Linda. "Respectful Death: A Model for End-of-life Care". Clinical Journal of Oncology Nursing 12(4) ;(August 2008): 621-626.

Watson R. "Luxembourg is to allow euthanasia from April 1." BMJ 338; (2009): b1248.

Wherry Aaron. "Assisted Suicide: What Will Parliament Do Now?" Macleans Magazine; (February 6, 2015); http://www.macleans.ca/politics/assisted-suicide-what-will-parliament-do-now/

Wilson K, Chochinov H, McPherson C, Skirko M, Allard P, Chary S, Clinch J, et al. "Desire for euthanasia or physician-assisted suicide in palliative cancer care." Health Psychology 26(3); (2007): 314-323. PsycArticles, EBSCOhost.

Wolfslast G. "Physician-assisted suicide and the German criminal law", in Dieter Birnbacher and Edgar Dahl (eds.*), Giving Death a Helping Hand: Physician-Assisted Suicide and Public Policy. An International Perspective*. New York: Springer, 2008.

World Federation of Right to Die Societies. "Is physician-assisted suicide the same as euthanasia?" Retrieved on July 5th 2015 from http://www.worldrtd.net/qanda/physician-assisted-suicide-same-euthanasia

World Health Organization. WHO Definition of Palliative Care. http://www.who.int/cancer/palliative/definition/en/

World Medical Association Resolution on Euthanasia, adopted in 2005, and reaffirmed in 2013. http://www.wma.net/en/30publications/10policies/e13b/

World Medical Ethics Manual 2nd Edition 2009. Chapter Two (pg.44) Retrieved from http://www.wma.net/en/30publications/30ethicsmanual/pdf/chap_2_en.pdf

Zachary RB. "Life with spina bifida." BMJ 01/1978; 2(6100). (1977): 1460–1462

BOOKS

McCaffery M and A Beebe. *Pain: Clinical Manual for Nursing Practice.* Toronto: C.V. Mosby, 1989,

Cicely Saunders, *The Management of Terminal Disease.* London: Edward Arnold, 1979.

Dowbiggin, Ian. *A Concise History of Euthanasia: Life, death, God, and Medicine* (Lanham, MD: Rowman & Littlefield, 2005).

Griffiths J, Bood A and H Weyers. *Euthanasia and Law in the Netherlands.* Amsterdam: Amsterdam University Press, 1998.

Neuman, Betty. *Neuman Systems Model: Application to Nursing Education and Practice.* Norwalk, CT: Appleton-Century-Crofts, 1982, p. 259.

Schadenberg, Alex. *Exposing Vulnerable People to Euthanasia and Assisted Suicide.* London, ON: Ross Lattner Educational Consultants, 2013.

Somerville, Margaret. *The Ethical Canary: Science, Society, and the Human Spirit.* Montreal: McGill-Queen's UP, 2004.

Van Loenen, Gerbert. *Do You Call This a Life? Blurred Boundaries in the Netherlands' Right-to-Die Laws.* London, ON: Ross Lattner Educational Consultants, 2015.

MEDIA/JOURNALS

Assisted-dying legislation in the UK. BBC Ethics Guide 2014. Retrieved from (http://www.bbc.co.uk/ethics/euthanasia/overview/asstdyingbill_1.shtml

Aviv R. "The Death Treatment." New Yorker. (June 22, 2015): pp. 56-63.

Beniuk, David. Tasmania's Euthanasia Bill fails. News (Oct.17, 2013). Retrieved from http://www.news.com.au/national/breaking-news/tasmanias-euthanasia-bill-fails-narrowly/story-e6frfku9-1226741999723

"Belgium Parliament Votes Through Child Euthanasia." BBC News.(February 13, 2014). http://www.bbc.com/news/world-europe-26181615. Accessed on August 4, 2015.

"Belgium passes law extending euthanasia to children of all ages". Guardian (2014, Feb.13) Retrieved from http://www.theguardian.com/world/2014/feb/13/belgium-law-extends-euthanasia-children-all-ages

"Colombia to Finalize Euthanasia Law in March ". Pan Am Post; (2015, February 19) Retrieved from http://panampost.com/sabrina-martin/2015/02/19/colombia-to-finalize-euthanasia-law-in-march/

Connolly John. "Luxembourg Parliament Passes Euthanasia Bill"; (2008, Feb.20) Retrieved from https://www.lifesitenews.com/news/luxembourg-parliament-passes-euthanasia-bill

Doughty S. "Don't make our mistake."   Daily Mail; (9 July 2014). http://www.dailymail.co.uk/news/article-2686711/Dont-make-mistake-As-assisted-suicide-bill-goes-Lords-Dutch-regulator-backed-euthanasia-warns-Britain-leads-mass-killing.html

Hall J. "She pushed for a legal right to die, and- thankfully- was rebuffed". Boston Globe; (October 4, 2011). http://www.boston.com/bostonglobe/editorial_opinion/letters/articles/2011/10/04/she_pushed_for_legal_right_to_die_and___thankfully___was_rebuffed/. Accessed July 29, 2015.

Harding S. "Letter Noting Assisted Suicide Raises Questions". KATU.com, July 30, 2008.http://www.katu.com/news/26119539.html

"House of Lords Debate Evenly Split Over Assisted Dying Legislation" Guardian; (2014, July 18) Retrieved from http://www.theguardian.com/society/2014/jul/18/assisted-dying-legalisation-debate-house-lords

James S. "Death Drugs Cause Uproar in Oregon." ABC News; (Aug. 8 2008). http://abcnews.go.com/Health/story?id=5517492

Montana Ruling Bolsters Doctor-Assisted Suicide. New York Times; (2009, Dec.31) Retrieved from http://www.nytimes.com/2010/01/01/us/01suicide.html

Kirkey, Sharon. "Confusion over euthanasia: Third of doctors wrongly believe it's family's call, Quebec poll finds". National Post. (23 April 2015); http://news.nationalpost.com/news/canada/confusion-over-euthanasia-third-of-doctors-wrongly-believe-its-familys-call-quebec-poll-finds

Kirkey, Sharon. National Post. "Panel to review assisted dying". (18 July 2015): A1.

Kirkey, Sharon. National Post. "Quebec MDs to get euthanasia packages" (1 Sept 2015): A1.

"PM David Cameron reaffirms opposition to assisted suicide and euthanasia" (June 23, 2015). https://www.youtube.com/watch?v=u8h_G3K-0vs

https://www.youtube.com/watch?v=u8h_G3K-0vsPonthus, J. "Luxembourg Parliament adopts euthanasia law." Reuters. (Feb. 20, 2008). Retrieved from http://www.reuters.com/article/2008/02/20/us-luxembourg-euthanasia-idUSL2011983320080220

Quebec health minister insists physicians, institutions must help patients seeking medical aid in dying. Canadian Press. September 3, 2015.

Sikkema, John. *Protecting Life: How Parliament Can Fully Ban Assisted Suicide without Section 33*. Ottawa: ARPA Canada, 2015.

Springer D. "Oregon Offers Terminal Patients Doctor-Assisted Suicide Instead of Medical Care." Fox News; (July 28, 2008). http://www.foxnews.com/story/2008/07/28/oregon-offers-terminal-patients-doctor-assisted-suicide-instead-medical-care/

Glossary

ADHD (Attention Deficit Hyperactivity Disorder): a common condition characterized by a constellation of temperamental traits such as impulsivity and 'absent-mindedness,' and a highly creative style of thinking often referred to 'out-of-the-box thinking.' It is estimated that 95% of successful inventors and entrepreneurs have ADHD. However, if metacognitive strategies to improve concentration and harness ones creative thoughts are not learned, persons with ADHD have a higher risk of school failure, drug and alcohol abuse and criminal activity.

Amyotrophic Lateral Sclerosis (ALS): commonly known as Lou Gerhig Disease after the famous base-ball player who was diagnosed with ALS while still playing major league ball. ALS causes the loss of voluntary striated muscle function due to the death of the nerve cells that control muscle growth and activity with the exception of the muscles that control the eyes.

Analgesics: medications that relieve pain. Analgesics are divided into two groups – narcotic analgesics and non-narcotic analgesics.

Anticonvulsants: medications that prevent or lessen the severity and frequency of convulsions (seizures).

Anxiety disorders: a group of mental disorders characterized by excessive amounts of anxiety that can manifest in various ways such as compulsive checking, panic attacks, incapacitating fear of a place, thing or activity as in a fear of flying. Anxiety disorders generally develop secondary to disordered family dynamics but may also result from acute mental, emotional or physical trauma/abuse.

Assisted Suicide: the act of taking one's own life with drugs and/or means prescribed or provided by a physician, who may or may not assist in the act.

Autism Spectrum Disorder: a complex array of disorders of brain development characterized by impaired development of social and communication skills. There is considerable variation in presentation from severely developmentally delayed individuals who are mute to highly successful university graduates that excel in visual arts, computer science and mathematics.

Benzodiazepine: a family of 'anti-anxiety' medications used to manage the debilitating side effects of anxiety. Benzodiazepines include such drugs as 'Ativan' and 'Xanax.' These drugs do not cure anxiety.

Bipolar disorder: also known as manic-depressive illness, is characterized by unusual and extreme shifts in mood, energy and activity levels that negatively affect a person's ability to carry out daily tasks. At either end of the spectrum (manic or depressed) a person can lose touch with reality and make irrational decisions or act in incomprehensible ways or indulge in high-risk behaviour.

Comatose: a mental state characterized by a decreased level of consciousness. The severity of a coma is assessed using the Glasgow Coma Scale which measures a person's best motor, eye, and verbal response.

Complicated grief: marked sadness over the loss of a loved one that lasts greater than six months and is associated with an increased risk of suicide due to a diminished ability to regulate emotions.

Continuous deep sedation: a form of treatment for severe, uncontrollable pain that renders the patient unconscious

and thus unaware of their pain, but is not intended
to hasten death by supressing respiration. However
in countries that have legalized euthanasia (Belgium,
Holland) the recorded direct cause of death in 25 to 30 per
cent of cases of euthanized patients is continuous deep
sedation.

Dementia: the loss of mental abilities, most notably the
loss of memory and good judgement that is accompanied
by structural changes of the brain. The most common
form of dementia is Alzheimer that initially presents with
short-term memory loss and disturbance of visual-spatial
planning.

Dissociative disorders: a sub-type of mental disorders
that range from a severe impairment in remembering
important information about one's self (dissociative
amnesia) to an inability to integrate one's experience into
one's understanding of self (depersonalization disorder)
to the totally dysfunctional state of not knowing oneself
or what one is doing while assuming the identity of
another (dissociative identity disorder). Most dissociative
disorders stem from living for extended periods of time in
abusive or traumatic environments (physical/sexual abuse
or prolonged torture as a prisoner of war).

Dysthymia: a mental condition marked by the absence
of joy, most often described as an indolent, low-
grade depression that lasts longer than two years. It
is often associated with poor eating habits, difficulties
sleeping, chronic fatigue, lethargy and a feeling of being
unappreciated and alone in the world.

Euthanasia: a medical act that results in the premature
death of a human being.

    Active euthanasia: an intentional act purportedly

to end suffering that causes the death of a human being.

Passive euthanasia: a misnomer that is used to describe death by natural causes following cessation of medical interventions that had been intentionally instituted to halt or slow the dying process.

Involuntary (non-voluntary) euthanasia: a medical act that intentionally ends a person's life without their consent.

Voluntary euthanasia: a medical act that intentionally ends a person's life with their consent.

Groningen Protocol: guidelines written by a group of doctors at the Groningen University Medical Centre in the Netherlands in 2005 for the termination of life in newborns and children up to age twelve. This includes newborns who are born with congenital anomaly, such as spina bifida, heart or kidney disease or children born with prematurity that lowers the quality of life and are medically deemed to have unbearable suffering.

Hydrocephalus: excessive collections of the fluid that circulates around the brain and spinal chord in the portion of the brain that produces the fluid due to a blockage of its outflow tract. This is corrected by a shunt (a flexible hollow silicone tube) that is inserted above the blockage site, then under the skin into the abdominal cavity. There is a valve that adjusts the flow of the fluid.

Informed consent: the agreement of a person who has a 'sound mind' to voluntarily undergo a particular medical act or treatment or investigation about which they have been fully informed.

Major depressive disorder: a mental illness that is characterized by feelings of being sad or empty accompanied by five of the following: insomnia; markedly diminished interest in one's activities; weight loss of > 5% of body weight; severe agitation or somnolence; lethargy; decreased ability to concentrate and make decisions; profound feelings of worthlessness; or thoughts of suicide; every day, all day, for more than two weeks.

Myelomeningocele (MMC): a developmental condition where the bones of the spine do not enclose the spinal chord (the nerves that connect the body to the brain). This defect occurs between the 3rd and 4th week of pregnancy and due to damage to the exposed spinal chord and nerves is often associated with paralysis of the lower limbs and incontinence of bowel and bladder.

Neuroleptic medications: medications that cause sedation and frequently prevent the person from remembering experienced pain or anxiety.

Obsessive-compulsive disorder: a severe debilitating type of personality disorder marked by obsessions and compensatory rituals such repeated washing of hands due to an obsession about germs.

Opioids: narcotic medications used to reduce or eliminate pain caused by injury to skin, muscle, bone or inner organs. Opioids are ineffective in the treatment of pain arising in damaged nerves.

Palliative care: compassionate care of the dying or chronically-ill person and to bring comfort to both the afflicted person and their loved ones.

Personality disorders: form a class of mental disorders that are characterized by long-lasting rigid patterns of thought and behaviour that impair functioning and cause serious problems in relationships.

Pervasive developmental disorders (PDD): refers to a group of disorders characterized primarily by delays in the development of socialization and communication skills accompanied by delays in development of fine motor skills and co-ordination.

Physician-assisted dying: an intentional act on the part of a physician that assists a person in ending their life otherwise known as physician-assisted suicide.

Post-traumatic stress disorder: an anxiety disorder, characterized by unmitigated fears that markedly limit a person's ability to function following a witnessed or experienced traumatic, terrifying event.

Psychotic disorders: are forms of mental illness characterized by disordered thought processes.

Schizophrenia: is a psychotic disorder characterized by hallucinations or delusions.

Sedatives: medications that evoke a feeling of calmness and frequently fatigue or sleepiness, and act to decrease anxiety, agitation or irritability.

Shunt (see hydrocephalus)

Somatoform disorder: a type of personality disorder characterized by physical symptoms that cannot be explained by an underlying disease process or injury.

Spina bifida: a birth defect that is most often related to insufficient folic acid in the mother's diet that results in a malformation of the backbone and spinal cord. There are three levels of severity: spina bifida occulta where the backbone does not fuse but the spinal chord is not damaged; meningocele where the lining tissue of the spinal chord extrudes through the non-fused bones of the spine and myelomeningocele where both the spinal chord (nerves) and the lining membranes extrude through the non-fused backbone.

Terminal illness: a disease process that will cause death.

Urinary catheterization: a small tube is inserted into a person's bladder through the urethra (the hole that one's urine comes out of) to drain urine. Generally this is required when a person has suffered an injury to the nerves that control the bladder as happens when a person is paralyzed or has Spina Bifida.

Withdrawal of Treatment: discontinuing a medical procedure or medication that is not providing any benefit to the person other than prolonging life (for example withdrawal of intravenous fluids).

Withholding of Treatment: not providing a medication or procedure that may benefit or prolong the life of a person.

Index

Active euthanasia, 24, 66, 71, 72, 74

ADHD (Attention Deficit Hyperactivity Disorder), 88

Albania, 51, 57, 63

ALS (Amyotrophic lateral sclerosis), 10, 21, 23, 101, 104, 106, 109, 126

An Act Respecting End-of-Life Care, 6, 16-7, 25, 69, 154

Analgesics, 74

Anticonvulsants, 74

Anxiety disorders, 87

Article, 5, 46, 61, 82, 131

Assisted Suicide, 1-11, 13-8, 21, 24, 26-8, 30-6, 39-67, 88-97, 99-113, 115, 117-20, 126-7, 132, 134, 138-9, 144, 148-50, 153, 155-6

Australia, 43-4

    Northern Territory Parliament, 43

Autism spectrum disorder, 88

Autonomy, 9, 27, 64, 94, 96, 100-3, 112, 115, 134, 150, 155

Belgium, 3, 7, 33, 51-2, 55-7, 62-3, 76, 78-89, 96-7, 111, 154, 156-7

Benzodiazepine, 110

Bipolar disorder, 87

Boer, Theo, 7, 64

British Columbia Court of Appeal, 20, 23

British Columbia Supreme Court, 22

British House of Lords, 7, 48

Canada, 1-3, 9, 11, 13-6, 20-6, 36, 39-40, 51, 62-3, 113-4, 117-8, 122, 140, 144-5

Canada (Attorney General) v Bedford, 23

Canadian Medical Association, 5, 13

Carter v Canada, 2, 9, 20, 22-3

Charter of Rights and Freedoms, 5, 26, 36, 118

Code of Ethics of Quebec Physicians, 12

Colombia, 20, 22-3, 28, 34, 39, 51-2, 57, 63

Comatose, 79

Complicated grief, 88

Continuous deep sedation, 68

Criminal Code of Canada:
9, 21
  section 14: 20-2, 26-7
  section 21: 22
  section 22: 22
  section 241: 11, 20-2, 126-7
Death With Dignity Act
  (Oregon/Washington), 34-5,
  58-60, 90-1, 93-5, 103
Dementia, 79, 142-3, 146
Depression, 13, 30-1, 64,
  69, 82-3, 86, 88, 94-5, 97, 99,
  105, 107-12, 116, 129, 147,
  153-4, 157   *See
  also Major depressive disorder*
Dignitas (Organization), 61
Dissociative disorder, 88
Dysthymia, 108
End-of-Life Decision Making,
  15, 81
Euthanasia, 3-20, 24, 28, 36,
  39-40, 43-8, 51-8, 60-74,
  76-89, 91-2, 96-7, 99-111, 113,
  115, 117-20, 126-7,
  130-4, 138-9, 144, 148-50,
  153-9
Euthanasia Society of
  America, 40
Exit (Organization), 61
Federal Medical Council
  (Bundesärztekammer), 41
France, 45-7
French National Assembly, 47

Germany, 39-40, 42-3
German Criminal Code, 42
German Ethics Council, 41
German Medical
  Association, 40-1
Gloria Taylor, 20-1, 23
Groningen Protocol, 70-3,75-6
House of Commons,
  British, 7, 51, 158
  Canadian, 24-5,
Hydrocephalus, 71
Involuntary euthanasia, 11
Jurist, 45
Latimer, Robert, 10-1
Lou Gehrig's Disease,
  See ALS
Luxembourg, 51-2, 56-7,
  63, 89
Major depressive disorder,
  87 *See also Depression*
MMC (Myelomeningocele),
  73-5
MS (Multiple Sclerosis), 126
Netherlands, 3, 7, 33, 51-5,
  57, 62-5, 67-71, 73, 82, 96-7,
  131, 144, 149, 151, 154, 156-8
Neuroleptic medications, 110
Nonvoluntary euthanasia,
  11, 72
Not Dead Yet UK
  (Organization), 50

Obsessive compulsive disorder, 88

Omission, 52, 139

Oregon, 34-5, 52, 55, 58-9, 62-3, 89-97, 101-3, 105-6, 156

Palliative care, 3, 7-8, 13-5, 19, 25, 34, 43, 61, 78, 82, 100, 106, 114-5, 117-135, 138-42, 148, 150-1, 153, 156, 158-9

Hospice(s), 6, 20, 114-5, 118-9, 121-4, 126-7, 129-33, 135, 139, 149, 153

Terminal, 69

Parliament, 9-10, 13-4, 16, 24-5, 36-7, 42-5, 47-8, 56, 86, 89, 113, 148, 150

Personality disorders, 83, 87

Pervasive developmental disorders, 87

Physician-assisted dying, 15, 22, 101

Private members' bills, 24-5, 45, 47

Psychotic disorders, 87

PTSD (Post-traumatic stress disorder), 87

Quebec, 6-7, 10, 12, 14, 16-20, 25-6, 67, 69, 153-5, 158

Referendum, 58, 90

Remmelink report, 63, 65-7

Rodriguez v British Columbia, 10, 27

Royal Society of Canada, 15-6

Schizophrenia, 87

Sedatives, 78

Select Committee on Dying with Dignity, 14-6

Senate of Canada, 11

Shunt, 75

Somatoform disorder, 87

Spina bifida, 71-6

Suicide, 1-29, 30-6, 39-55, 57-67, 82, 88, 89-97, 99-115, 117-120 126-7, 132, 134, 138-9, 144, 146, 148-50, 153, 155-9

Suicide prevention, 34, 61, 111, 114, 144, 148

Supreme Court of Canada (SCC), 2, 9, 20, 23, 36, 118, 155

Switzerland, 21, 57-8, 61-3, 88-9

Terminal illness, 55, 59, 69, 80, 122, 124, 130-1

United States, 39, 58, 92

Vermont, 52, 58, 60, 62-3, 89-90

Voluntary Euthanasia, 11

Washington, 35, 52, 58-9, 62-3, 89-90, 95-7, 103, 156